Landscapes of
MADEIRA

a countryside guide
Sixth edition

John and Pat Underwood

SUNFLOWER BOOKS

For José Fernandes
*who urged us to see more
of his island and so quite
changed our lives!*

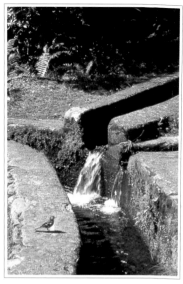

Sixth edition
Copyright © 2000
Sunflower Books™
12 Kendrick Mews
London SW7 3HG, UK

ISBN 1-85691-161-6

Levada do Furado (Walk 25)

Important note to the reader

We have tried to ensure that the descriptions and maps in this book are error-free at press date. **Be sure to write to us for an 'Update' before you travel** (see inside back cover). It is very helpful for us to receive your comments (sent in care of the publishers, please) for the updating of future printings.

We rely on those who use this book — especially walkers — to take along a good supply of common sense when they explore. Conditions change very rapidly on Madeira, and **storm damage or bulldozing may make a route unsafe at any time.** If the route is not as we outline it here, and your way ahead is not secure, return to the point of departure. **Never attempt to complete a tour or walk under hazardous conditions!** Please read carefully the notes on pages 35 to 40, the Country code on page 8, and the introductory comments at the beginning of each tour and walk (regarding road conditions, equipment, grade, distances and time, etc). Explore **safely**, while at the same time respecting the beauty of the countryside.

Cover photograph: Levada da Rocha Vermelha (Walk 37)
Title page: the peaks from the ER104 near Rosário
Photographs: John Underwood
Maps: John Underwood, adapted from Portuguese IGC/military maps;
   see 'Acknowledgements', page 7
A CIP catalogue record for this book is available from the British Library.
Printed and bound in the UK by Brightsea Press, Exeter

10 9 8 7 6 5 4 3

● Contents _____

Preface   5
  The levadas   5
  Acknowledgements; Recommended reading   7

A country code for walkers and motorists   8

Getting about   9
  Plan of Funchal city centre   10-11
    with city exits and bus departure points

Picnicking   12
  Picnic suggestions   12

Touring   17
  1 MADEIRA NORTH AND SOUTH   18
  2 EASTERN MADEIRA'S GENTLE CHARMS   21
  3 THE CORRAL AND THE CAPE   24
  4 MOUNTAINS AND MORE MOUNTAINS!   26
  5 PORTO MONIZ AND THE PAÚL DA SERRA   30
  6 THE SUNNY SOUTHWEST COAST   33

Walking   35
  Guides, waymarking, maps   35
  Where to stay   36
  Weather   37
  What to take   38
  Nuisances   38
  Portuguese for walkers   39
  Organisation of the walks   40

  FUNCHAL AND THE SOUTHEAST
  1 The Socorridos Valley: Levada dos Piornais and
    Levada do Curral   41
  2 From the Poço da Neve to Barreira   45
  3 From the Eira do Serrado to Curral   47
  4 Boca da Corrida • Pico Grande • Encumeada   49
  5 Fontes • Achada da Pinta • Trompica • Fontes   51
  6 Levada do Norte: from Estreito de Câmara de Lobos
    to Barreiras   54
  7 Levada dos Tornos: from Romeiros to the
    Sítio das Quatro Estradas   59
  8 Camacha • Levada do Caniço • Assomada   67
  9 Santo da Serra • Levada Nova • Sítio das Quatro Estradas   68
  10 Levada da Serra: from Choupana to Portela   70
  11 Levada do Caniçal: from Maroços to the Caniçal tunnel   72
  12 Pico do Facho — Caniçal circuit   74
  13 Ponta de São Lourenço   76

  THE NORTHEAST AND THE GREAT PEAKS
  14 North coast path: Caniçal tunnel • Boca do Risco •
    Porto da Cruz   79
  15 From Portela to Porto da Cruz   83

16 Cruz • Levada do Castelejo • Cruz   84
17 Penha de Águia   85
18 Santana • São Jorge • Vigia   87
19 Pico do Arieiro • Pico Ruivo • Achada do Teixeira   89
20 Achada do Teixeira • Pico Ruivo • Torrinhas •
    Encumeada   92
21 Pico das Pedras • Cova da Roda • Cruzinhas   95
22 Queimadas • Levada do Caldeirão Verde • Santana   97
23 Queimadas • Caldeirão do Inferno • Queimadas   100
24 Fajã da Nogueira   102
25 Levada do Furado: Ribeiro Frio • Lamaceiros • Portela   104
26 Pico do Suna   107
27 Circuit above Boaventura   109
28 Queimadas • Vale da Lapa • Ilha de São Jorge   111

THE WEST AND NORTHWEST
29 Levada da Fajã do Rodrigues   112
30 Lombada da Ponta do Sol • Levada Nova • Tabua •
    Ribeira Brava   113
31 Encumeada • Levada do Lombo do Mouro •
    Ribeira Brava   115
32 Folhadal and the Norte and Rabaças levadas   117
33 Bica da Cana • Levada da Serra • Pináculo •
    Bica da Cana   119
34 Fanal   121
35 Campo Grande • Levada do Paúl • Rabaçal • Loreto   122
36 Cascalho   126
37 Rabaçal's levadas   128
38 Levada da Ribeira Grande   131
39 Pico Ruivo do Paúl   132
40 From Prazeres to Paúl do Mar   133
41 Levada Calheta–Ponta do Pargo   134
42 Levada da Central da Ribeira da Janela   136

Bus timetables   138

Index (of geographical names)   143
    Pronunciation/translation of some index entries   144

Touring map   *inside back cover*

Pico Grande from the flanks of Pico do Arieiro

• Preface

Since we first published a small book of Madeira walks in 1980, not only has *Landscapes of Madeira* become the most widely-used guide on the island, but it inspired a whole series of *Landscapes* books, which we publish under our Sunflower imprint. The aim of the series is to lead the visitor off the beaten track and into the countryside — whether by car, public transport, or on foot.

Many changes have come about since the last edition of this book was published just a few years ago. In this Sixth edition, we have dropped one of the strenuous 'classic' hikes: in our opinion, new roads at the start and finish made it too short to compensate for the effort involved. In its place, two completely new, easy walks are described. Moreover we have added many new alternatives — some of them walks in their own right — and, where possible, described more circuits for motorists. *The most important change, however, is the new maps:* John has redrawn them all, and we hope you will find them more 'user-friendly' on the ground.

All Sunflower authors hope to convey more than mere enthusiasm for their chosen landscapes — love might be a better word. Our love affair with Madeira really came into blossom with our 'discovery' of the levadas. They never cease to fascinate or inspire us. No matter how tired we may be, to walk beside a levada always refreshes our spirits and brings the bounce back into our steps.

The levadas

Whether you use this book to tour, walk or picnic, we will lead you along the levadas. Such watercourses are not unique to Madeira: what *is* unique is their **accessibility** and **extent**. You need only venture a little way off the main roads to begin to appreciate Madeira's myriad aqueducts — for their beauty, ingenuity of design, and for the courage and determination needed to bring the concept to its present glory. The island's irrigation system now comprises an impressive 2150km (1350 miles) of channels, including 40km (25 miles) of tunnels — and the work started centuries ago.

The earliest settlers on Madeira began cultivating the lower slopes in the south of the island, cutting out small terraces like those shown on page 7 *(poios)*. Working with contractors (who sometimes used slave or convict labour), they built the first small levadas, which carried water from springs higher up the mountainsides to irrigate their lands.

Tiny streams feed the Levada da Negra (Walk 2).

These narrow watercourses (see left) plummet downhill, rushing and frothing with energy; their banks are often festooned with wild flowers.

By the early 1900s, there were about 200 of these levadas, meandering over about 1000km (620 miles). Many were privately owned, and the undisciplined appropriation of water meant that the island's most valuable asset was often unfairly distributed. In fact, by the mid 1930s, only two-thirds of the island's arable land was under cultivation — and just half of that was irrigated. Only the State had the money to implement a major building programme and the authority to enforce a more equitable system of distribution.

For there was plenty of water for irrigation, and torrents to spare for power. Clouds driven to the island by the prevailing northerly winds are caught by the central mountain chain, and as much as 2m (80 inches) of rain may fall in the north in a year, while the south coast may be relatively dry for up to six months. In effect the island is a huge self-regulating reservoir. Rain seeps down into the porous volcanic ash but, on meeting impervious layers of rock, it wells up again in springs. Unless this rainwater is channelled, it just runs down ravines and into the sea.

In 1939 the Portuguese government sent a mission to the island to study a combined irrigation/hydroelectric scheme. The 'new' levadas created from its plans — wide mini-canals — contour through the valleys; their flow is stately and serene, and their banks are lovingly planted with agapanthus lilies and hydrangeas. These wide waterways are first channelled out at an altitude of about 1000m/3300ft, where the concentration of rainfall, dew and springs is greatest. The water is then piped down to the power stations lying just at the outer edge of the arable land (about 600m/2000ft), from where it flows on to the irrigated zones. Here, distribution is carried out by the *levadeiro,* who diverts the flow to each proprietor.

Most of the mission's development plans were imple-

Terraces (poios) in the Ribeira dos Socorridos (Walk 1, Picnic 1)

mented by 1970. Among the most important projects were the Levada do Norte and the Levada dos Tornos, both of which you will discover as you tour, walk or picnic. Their incredible length, considering the terrain, is best gauged on the fold-out touring map. The work took only 25 years to complete, although it was all done by hand. How were the tunnels cut through the solid basalt? How did the workers channel out the levadas beneath the icy waterfalls, halfway between earth and sky? Often, as during the construction of the corniche road between São Vicente and Porto Moniz, they were suspended from above in wicker baskets, while they fought the unyielding stone with picks. Many lost their lives to bring water and electricity to the islanders ... and unending joy to walkers.

Acknowledgements

We are very grateful for the invaluable help of the following people:
Luís de Sousa and John Blandy, for guiding; Richard Blandy, for introducing us to the *Elucidario,* a three-volume compendium of island history; the Instituto Geográfico e Cadastral, for permission to adapt their maps; Ton van der Velden, Clive Scott, Aníbal Jesus Rodrigues, and Jorge Nóbrega for special help with this Sixth edition; Raimundo Quintal, for encouraging young people to protect their island's heritage; and the hundreds of 'Landscapers' who write to us with Update information.

Recommended reading

There are now several good general guides available.

The Madeira Book, by John and Pat Underwood (Sunflower Books) is the most complete picture of present-day Madeira in print and an ideal companion volume to *Landscapes of Madeira.* Among the subjects described and illustrated with 350 colour photographs are: the volcanic nature of the land, terracing and the levadas, island crafts and industries, housing, festivals, gardens and parks, legends, historical figures associated with Madeira, architecture, and island walks.

Madeira: Plants and Flowers, by Luís Franquinho and António da Costa (distributed by Sunflower Books) is the most comprehensive guide to the island's flora available. More than 400 plants are identified and illustrated with 700 colour photographs.

A country code for walkers and motorists

The experienced rambler is used to following a 'country code', but the tourist out for a lark may unwittingly cause damage, harm animals, and even endanger his own life. Please respect this country code.

■ **Only light fires at purpose-built fireplaces.**

■ **Do not damage levadas.** Don't touch sluice gates or the stones used to control small sluices.

■ **Protect all wild and cultivated plants.** Don't pick wild flowers or saplings. Never cross cultivated land!

■ **Take all your litter away with you.**

■ **Do not frighten animals.** They are not tame. By making loud noises, or trying to touch or photograph them, you may cause them to run in fear — over a precipice.

■ **Leave all gates as you find them.** They have a purpose: generally to keep animals in — or out of — an area.

■ **Walkers — DO NOT TAKE RISKS!** And remember:

— **At any time a walk may become unsafe.** If the route is not as we describe it, if mists are falling, or if it is late in the day, *turn back!* Remember, there is *virtually no twilight on Madeira!*

— **NEVER walk alone** — and **always** tell a responsible person *exactly* where you are going and what time you plan to return.

— **Do not overestimate your capacity:** your speed will be determined by the slowest walker in the group, and bus connections may be vital.

— **Proper footwear is essential.** Flat clay paths can be deceptive; when they are damp they can be as slippery as ice.

— **Mists can fall suddenly** on the Paúl da Serra and in the mountains.

— **Warm clothing** and **extra rations** are needed in the mountains.

— **Compass, whistle, torch, first-aid kit** weigh little, but might save your life. If you become lost or injure yourself, it may be a very long time before you are found, and there are *no* official rescue services.

— **Protect yourself from the sun.**

— **A stout stick** is a help on steep terrain and to discourage the rare unfriendly dog (see also note on page 38, 'Nuisances').

— **Read and re-read the 'Important note'** on page 2 and guidelines on grade and equipment for each walk you plan to do.

Ancient laurels in the Fanal (Walk 34)

⚘ Getting about ___

There is no doubt that a **hired car** or taxi is the most convenient way of getting round the island. We hope that the liberal cross-references to picnics and walks in the touring section will inspire motorists and walkers to team up on car hire. The walking maps show the car symbol (🚗) only at the *parking* places we recommend in the text; if friends can drop you off or collect you, look on the maps for places where roads cross the walks.

All **taxi** drivers carry a government-approved price list for journeys outside Funchal. *Don't be afraid to bargain, however.* Your hotel porter may be able to suggest a driver for an all-day tour: some are especially knowledgeable about island culture and customs; a few are keen walkers.

Coach tours are the most popular way of 'seeing Madeira in a day'. They provide a painless introduction to road conditions and a remarkable overview of island scenery. You'll discover in comfort the landscapes you'll want to explore at leisure, on your own.

Our favourite way of getting about is by **bus**. The system is economical, reliable, and fun! You get splendid views perched up on bus seats, and most of the buses are new and quite comfortable. The drivers are expert; we always feel safe in their hands. The town plan on the following pages shows you where to board your bus in Funchal. The two largest operators, SAM and Rodoeste, have bus stations. While SAM's is fairly convenient, Rodoeste's is *not!* But most people catch SAM and Rodoeste buses at their main departure points on the Avenida do Mar (see plan) and buy tickets on the bus. Other 'country' bus tickets (EACL, AC, SR do Faial) are usually bought at the operators' kiosks near the bus departure points. For orange town buses, fare-saving tickets are available: see notes at the top of page 142. (By the way, don't be confused by identical bus numbers, eg orange town bus 20 to Monte; green/cream country bus 20 to Santo da Serra.)

Please do not rely *solely* on our **bus timetables** (pages 138-142); changes are fairly frequent. You can update our timetables at the Tourist Office on Avenida Arriaga or, better still, at the various operators' bus stations or kiosks. *Do arrive early for your bus!* It may take you several minutes to find the one you want, and they leave spot on time!

1	Tourist Office	20	Municipal Museum
2	Infante Fountains	21	Post Office, SAM Bus Station
3	Blandy Agency	22	São Lourenço Palace
4	Air Portugal (TAP)	23	Collegiate Church
5	Municipal Theatre	24	Madeira Wine Institute
6	Casa do Turista	25	Law Courts
7	Government Offices	26	Town Hall
8	Sé (Cathedral)	27	Museum of Sacred Art
9	Regional Parliament	28	New Customs House
10	Old Customs House	29	Market
11	Shopping Centre	30	Forte de São Tiago
12	Santa Caterina Chapel	31	Old Town
13	Quinta Vigia (President's House)	32	Boat Trips
14	Casino	33	Museum of Electricity
15	Hospital	34	Praça da Autonomia
16	Barreiros Stadium	35	Rodoeste Bus Station
17	Forte do Pico	36	Beatles' Boat
18	Quinta das Cruzes	37	Banger Pillar
19	Santa Clara Convent	38	parking area; 🚕 taxi rank

BUS DEPARTURES

N°	Destination		*from*	Company (and Livery)
2	Assomada		**38**	EACL (grey/red)
3	Estreito de C. de Lobos		**22**	Rodoeste (cream/red)
4	Madalena do Mar		**22**	Rodoeste (cream/red)
6	Boaventura via ER104		**22**	Rodoeste (cream/red)
7	Ribeira Brava		**22**	Rodoeste (cream/red)
20	Santo da Serra	*opposite*	**9**	SAM (cream/green)
23	Machico	*opposite*	**9**	SAM (cream/green)
25	Santo da Serra	*opposite*	**9**	SAM (cream/green)

Funchal

N

0   250m   500m

1/4 mi

N°	Destination		from	Company (and Livery)
29	Camacha		38	AC (white/yellow/silver)
53	Faial, Igreja	opposite	9	SAM (cream/green)
60	Boqueirão	opposite	9	SAM (cream/green)
77	Santo da Serra		38	AC (white/yellow/silver)
78	Machico, Faial	opposite	9	SAM (cream/green)
81	Curral das Freiras		38	AC (white/yellow/silver)
96	Corticeiras, Foro		22	Rodoeste (cream/red)
103	Boaventura via ER103		38	SR do Faial (cream/red)
107	Raposeira		22	Rodoeste (cream/red)
110	Boqueirão		38	AC (white/yellow/silver)
111	Achadinha		38	AC (white/yellow/silver)
113	Machico, Caniçal	opposite	9	SAM (cream/green)
114	Nogueira		38	AC (white/yellow/silver)
115	Estreito da Calheta		22	Rodoeste (cream/red)
123	Campanário		22	Rodoeste (cream/red)
138	São Jorge (Cabanas)		38	SR do Faial (cream/red)
139	Porto Moniz		22	Rodoeste (cream/red)
142	Ponta do Pargo		22	Rodoeste (cream/red)
148	Boa Morte		22	Rodoeste (cream/red)
154	Cabo Girão		22	Rodoeste (cream/red)
155	Ponta da Oliveira		38	EACL (grey/red)
156	Machico, Maroços	opposite	9	SAM (cream/green)

ORANGE TOWN BUSES (Horarios do Funchal)

1, 3	Lombada		33	29	Romeiros	east of	33
2	Quebradas		33	30	Jardim Botânico	east of	33
8, 16	Santa Quitéria		28	36, 37	Palheiro Ferreiro	east of	33
11	Trapiche		28	45	Stadium	opposite	6
20, 21	Monte	north of	34	47	São João Latrão	east of	33
22	Babosas	east of	33	ⓘ	town and AC bus information		

11

● Picnicking

In the course of some of our rambles we've come upon easy-to-reach picnic spots that might appeal to those of you who prefer *very* short walks. If you are car touring, they are an 'off-the-beaten-track' alternative to the island's many road-side picnic tables.

All the information you need to find these more secluded picnic spots is given below, where *picnic numbers correspond to walk numbers,* so that you can quickly find the general location on the island by looking at the touring map (where walks are highlighted in green). We give you walking times and transport details. The location of the picnic is indicated by the symbol *P* on the appropriate *walking map,* which also shows the nearest 🚌 stop (if appropriate) and 🚗 parking area. Most of the picnic settings are illustrated.

Please remember to **wear sensible shoes and take a sunhat** (the symbol ○ after the title indicates a picnic **in full sun**). It's a good idea to take along a plastic groundsheet as well, in case it's damp or prickly.

If you are travelling by bus, check the latest schedules shown in the kiosks in Funchal (see page 9). **Travelling by car**, park *well off* the road; *never* block a road or track.

All picnickers should read the Country code on page 8 and go quietly in the countryside.

1 SOCORRIDOS VALLEY (map page 43, photograph page 7)

🚗 or town 🚌 1 or 3 to Lombada. By car take the northbound road 1km east of Câmara de Lobos, signposted 'Pico dos Barcelos'; park 0.7km north. **10-20min on foot.** *From the bus stop walk uphill to a Y-fork and bear right up the Vereda do Pico da Lombada. Cross a bridge over the motorway, then turn left on the Levada dos Piornais for about 10 minutes.* **Picnic just before the tunnels on one of the grassy verges, out of sight (and earshot!) of the stone-sorting works below, but with lovely views.**

2 POÇO DA NEVE, ARIEIRO (map on reverse of touring map, photograph opposite) ○

🚗 ice house (Poço da Neve); it lies *below* the road, hidden by a stone wall edging a small parking bay, 2km below Pico do Arieiro (Car tours 1, 4). **Up to 5min on foot.** *Picnic by the ice house (no shade), or below it in the heath tree grove.* **Splendid view over moors, down to Funchal.**

3 EIRA DO SERRADO (map on reverse of touring map, photograph pages 46-47)

🚗 (Car tour 3) to the Eira do Serrado. **5min on foot.** Or 🚌 81 to the Eira turn-off on the ER107. **20min on foot.** *Follow Walk 3 (pages 47-48) from the 15min-point for five minutes.* **Fine view over Curral, away from the crowds.**

The Santa Luzia Valley and Funchal from the Poço da Neve ('snow pit' or 'ice house'). Walk and Picnic 2; Car tours 1 and 4

6 BOA MORTE (map page 54, photograph page 56)

🚌 or 🚐 127 to Boa Morte. By car, take the northbound road to 'S João/ S Paulo' (at the KM172 stone on the ER229; Car tour 6). Continue past Boa Morte to the Levada do Norte (3.5km from the ER229), where you can park. **Up to 25min on foot.** By bus follow Short walk 6-3, page 54, returning on 🚐 148. **Up to 35min on foot.** *Turn left (northwest) on the levada. **The forest itself is an exceptionally lovely setting, or continue on the levada to the valley overlook, for magnificent views of the Ribeira Brava and the Paúl da Serra. Good shade.***

7a PORTO NOVO FROM THE EAST (map pages 62-63)

🚌 or 🚐 60 (Boqueirão bus) to the Levada dos Tornos. **15-20min on foot.** By car, take the ER206 south from Águas Mansas (Car tour 2) and park by the levada, 1.6km downhill. By bus, ask the driver for 'Levada dos Tornos, Lombo Grande'; the levada is a minute uphill from the stop. *Head west on the levada: 10 minutes' walking will give you good views, or go as far as the tunnel with 'windows' mentioned on page 64 (20min). **This picnic overlooks the western side of the Porto Novo Valley and is at its best in spring. Some shade nearby.***

7b BOAVENTURA VALLEY (map pages 62-63, photograph page 66)

🚌 and 🚐 as 7a above. **30min on foot.** *Follow the notes for Short walk 7-4, page 65. **Overlook a golden valley (at its best in summer) and the south coast. Some shade.***

8 PORTO NOVO FROM THE WEST (map pages 62-63, photo page 16)

🚌 or 🚐 2, etc to Assomada. By car, drive up the road on the east side of the church and its parking lot (Car tour 2). Bear left *and left again* to pass an electricity sub-station on your left (a squarish grey building, easily seen from the ER204). After 1km uphill, watch for a water trough on your right, raised up on pillars (an old mill-race). Park here, well tucked in. **10-15min on foot.** By bus, use notes for motorists above. **30-35min on foot.** *Follow the path at the left of the raised mill-race up to the Levada do Caniço, then turn right. **You overlook the eastern escarpment of the valley and São Lourenço. The setting is ideal for an early evening picnic.***

These rocks off the north coast of the Ponta de São Lourenço seem almost fluorescent (Car tour 2, Walk and Picnic 13)

10 LEVADA DA SERRA
(map page 62,
photograph page 21)

🚶 or 🚌 77 to the Sítio das Quatro Estradas, where the ER202 joins the ER102. By car, head west towards Poiso and park by the levada after 0.5km, just past the piggery (Car tours 2, 4). **7min on foot.** By bus, follow Short walk 10-4, page 71. **22min on foot.** *Head north on the levada and picnic about seven minutes along, under oaks and beside summer-blooming hydrangeas.* **No far-reaching views, just a lovely setting.**

11 LEVADA DO CANIÇAL (map page 81)

🚶 (Car tour 2) or 🚌 113 to the 'Pico do Facho' bus stop. Motorists should park at the start of the road to Pico do Facho, well tucked in. **20-30min on foot.** *Follow Short walk 11, page 72, for only 20-30min.* **Picnic on grassy verges in full sun, or in the shade of mimosas.**

13 ABRA BAY (map pages 76-77, photographs above and page 78) ○

🚶 (Car tour 2) or 🚌 113 *(summer only)* to the Abra Bay viewpoint (🏞), at the end of the ER109. **Up to 20min on foot.** *Picnic at the viewpoint or follow Walk 13 (page 76) for 15-20min.* **Magnificent coastal views, but no shade.**

15 PORTELA (map pages 80-81, photograph pages 82-83)

🚶 (Car tour 4) or 🚌 20, 53 or 78 to Portela. **5min on foot.** *Follow Walk 15 (page 83) for 5min; if you like, continue further east along the track.* **Superb view over Penha de Águia, away from the coaches. Shade.**

16 LEVADA DO CASTELEJO (map page 105, photograph pages 84-85)

🚶 (Car tour 4) or 🚌 53 or 78 to Cruz. **Up to 30min on foot.** *Follow Walk 16 (page 84).* **You can look out towards Penha de Águia (20min) or up to the high peaks (25-30min). Shade nearby.**

19 PICO DO ARIEIRO (map on reverse of touring map, photograph pages 90-91) ○

🚶 Pico do Arieiro (Car tours 1, 4). **Up to 15min on foot.** *Picnic near the start of Walk 19, on a grassy verge before the first viewpoint (notes page 90).* **Stupendous mountain setting and views. No shade.**

20 ACHADA DO TEIXEIRA (map on reverse of touring map, photograph page 93)

🚶 Achada do Teixeira (Car tour 4). **5-50min on foot.** *Picnic at Homem* *em Pé (the basaltic dyke just below the house; 5min; shade), or follow Short walk 20 (page 92) to picnic on the Ruivo path or at Pico Ruivo itself (50min).* **Lacks the drama of Picnic 19, but the settings and views are fabulous.**

22 QUEIMADAS (map pages 98-99, photograph page 97)

🚌 Queimadas Park or the Rancho Pico das Pedras on the ER218: see Car tour 4, page 27. **Up to 35min on foot.** *Picnic by the Queimadas houses, or explore the Levada do Caldeirão Verde (see Short walks, page 97).* **No far-reaching views, but a fairytale setting.**

25 BALCÕES (map page 105, similar view page 108, top)

🚌 (Car tours 1, 4) or 🚌 103 or 138 to Ribeiro Frio. **20min on foot.** *Follow the Short walk on page 104.* **Superb outlook over the central peaks, the Metade Valley and Fajã da Nogueira. Shade nearby.**

31 LOMBO DO MOURO (map on reverse of touring map, photographs page 116, similar views on pages 117, 119)

🚌 to the parking bay above the Lombo do Mouro house, signposted on the ER110 between Encumeada and Bica da Cana (Car tours 5, 6). **10-15min on foot.** *Descend the steps to the house, then turn right a short way along the levada.* **Superb views east to the peaks and west to the escarpment of the Paúl da Serra; rushing levada; nearby shade.**

32 LAPA DO GALHO (map on reverse of touring map, nearby photograph page 117, right)

🚌 or 🚌 6 to Encumeada. Park at the viewpoint on the north side of the pass (Car tours 1, 5, 6). **10-15min on foot.** *Climb steps opposite the bar/restaurant on the south side of the pass, to join the Levada do Norte (signposted 'Folhadal'). Lapa do Galho, a fine promontory, is 12min from the road (2min before the first tunnel).* **Wonderful views to the great peaks; wealth of vegetation on the levada. Shade nearby.**

33 BICA DA CANA (map on reverse of touring map, photograph page 119)

🚌 at the entrance (with two concrete pillars) to the house (Car tours 5, 6). **Up to 10min on foot.** *Follow the track towards the Bica house and then up to the triangulation point/miradouro (no shade).* **Stupendous views of the great peaks. Plenty of shade in the surrounding area.**

From a pine-shaded bench below Prazeres, you look out towards some of the most fascinating coastal cliffs on the island (Walk and Picnic 40, detour on Car tour 6).

The afternoon sun paints the eastern escarpment of the Porto Novo ravine the colour of burnished copper (Picnic 8).

35 and 36 LEVADA DO PAÚL/LEVADA DA BICA DA CANA
(map pages 124-125, photographs pages 122, 126-127) ○

🚗 by the waterhouse on the ER209, below the statue of Cristo Rei, 9km north of Canhas (Car tours 5, 6). **Up to 45min on foot.** *Follow the Levada do Paúl to the west (Walk 35, page 122; no shade) or the Levada da Bica da Cana to the east (Walk 36, page 126; a lone pine provides shade). Suggested picnic spots are described in the walking notes.* **Fine views over the south coast, beside a mesmerising ribbon of levada.**

37a-e RABAÇAL (map pages 124-125, photograph page 129)

🚗 Rabaçal (Car tours 5, 6). *The road to Rabaçal is very vertiginous. You can also park on the ER211, from where you can walk to Rabaçal in 30 minutes: see notes for Alternative walk 37-1, page 128;* **torch essential. Up to 50min on foot** *from Rabaçal. There are five picnic choices: (a) by the Rabaçal houses; (b) a sun-trap below the houses, at the Rabaçal end of the tunnel (follow Short walk 37-2 down to the Levada das 25 Fontes and turn left); (c) far side of the tunnel, overlooking Calheta's valley (follow (b), then continue past the sun-trap and through the tunnel* — **torch essential***); (d) Risco waterfall (Short walk 37-1); (e) 25 Fontes (Short walk 37-2).* **All these settings are lovely and have ample shade.**

38 LEVADA DA RIBEIRA GRANDE (map pages 124-125)

🚗 at the parking area on the ER110, at the top of the road to Rabaçal (Car tours 5, 6). **12min on foot.** *Follow Walk 38 (page 131) to the pretty little reservoir.* **No views, but a lovely shady setting on a hot day.**

39 BELOW PICO RUIVO DO PAÚL (map page 132, photographs pages 34 and 132)

🚗 at the junction of the ER110 to Bica da Cana and the road to Estanquinhos, by a small levada (Car tours 5, 6). **Up to 20min on foot.** *Follow Walk 39 (page 132) for as long as you like.* **Beautiful views across the Paúl da Serra and its miniature 'red peak'. Plenty of shade.**

40 PRAZERES (map page 134, photograph page 15)

🚗 or 🚌 80, 107 or 142 to Prazeres. By car (detour on Car tour 6), park at the Hotel Jardim Atlántico. **10min on foot.** By bus, walk 2km down to the hotel. **40min on foot.** *From the hotel follow Walk 40 (page 133) for just over 10min.* **Dramatic views to the sea and the steeply-terraced cliffs west of Prazeres.**

42 LEVADA DA CENTRAL DA RIBEIRA DA JANELA
(map page 137, photograph page 136)

🚗 at the reservoir above Porto Moniz (Car tour 5). See 'How to get there', page 136. **3-30min on foot.** *Use the notes for Walk 42 (page 136); picnic by the first filtration point (3min; 🚌) or the second (30min).* **Fantastic views of the great Janela Valley; picturesque levada. Good shade.**

Touring

Car touring on the island has become a real pleasure for us, thanks to the new roads and expressways. From Funchal we can now be on the Paúl da Serra in 45 minutes — a drive that used to take about three hours! But once you are off the expressways, driving on the older, winding country roads can be quite tiring and time-consuming: you are unlikely to average more than about 20km/h. So plan leisurely excursions if possible, with walking breaks to stretch your legs. **The best one-day excursion is Car tour 1; Car tours 4 and 5 (or 6) make an ideal two-day programme.**

In the touring and walking notes we often refer to **road numbers**. *This is to help you with orientation when using our maps,* since at time of writing there was virtually no sign-posting of route numbers. Hopefully money will be found to do this in the next few years. Although almost all roads are now asphalted, *beware of pot-holes and, on some roads, deep ditches at the sides.* In the southeast there is still quite a bit of road-building going on, and you are likely to become caught up behind container and road construction lorries.

Our touring notes are brief: they include little history or information that can be found in a general guide or in *The Madeira Book* (see page 7). We concentrate instead on the 'logistics' of touring: times and distances, road conditions, getting to the best viewpoints at the right time of day, etc. Most of all, we emphasise possibilities for **walking** and **picnicking**. If you're picnicking or sharing a car with walkers, you should find the 🚗 symbols on the walking maps useful: these alert you to places where you can park near a walk. And *do* refer to these walking maps from time to time while touring — perhaps when you stop at a viewpoint; they contain far more information than the touring map.

The large fold-out touring map is designed to be held out opposite the touring notes. City exits correspond to those on the plan on pages 10-11. **Symbols** used in the text are explained in the map key.

Take along **warm clothing, food** and **drink**; you may experience delays, even on main roads. **Allow ample time for stops**: our times include only short breaks at viewpoints labelled 🕰 in the notes. Calculate time for **detours** as well: places, picnics and walks shown in ( ) are only accessible via detours off the main route.

All motorists should read the Country code on page 8 and go quietly in the countryside. *Boa viagem!*

1 MADEIRA NORTH AND SOUTH

Funchal • Encumeada • São Vicente • (Porto Moniz) •
Boaventura • Santana • Faial • Ribeiro Frio • Poiso • (Pico
do Arieiro) • Monte • Funchal

*113km/70mi; 5-6 hours' driving **without detours** (add 31km/19mi; 2h
for the detour to Porto Moniz and 14km/9mi; 1h for the detour to Pico
do Arieiro); take the nearest expressway exit from Funchal.*

On route: ⌂ at Vinháticos, Encumeada, Chão dos Louros, above
Rosário, Ponta Delgada, Boaventura, ER103 around Ribeiro Frio, Pico
do Arieiro; Picnics (see **P** symbol and pages 12-16): (2, 19, 22), 25, 32,
(42); Walks (2), 5, (7), 10, 18, 20, 21, 22, (23, 24), 25, 27, (28, 29), 31,
32, (42)

*If you have only one day to tour the island, then this is the circuit to do,
including the detours to Porto Moniz and Pico do Arieiro. Leave
Funchal **very** early in the morning; we've planned the tour so that you
have the best views westwards in the morning and to the east in the
afternoon. If, however, you have a car for several days, then do Tours
4 and 5 (or 6) **instead of** this long expedition. The roads are mostly good,
but some stretches on the north coast are narrow and frequented by tour
coaches; you may be forced to back up to let them pass.*

From Funchal take the expressway west (Via Rápida; ER1),
quickly whizzing across the lovely 'winged' bridge over
the Socorridos. Ignore exits for Cabo Girão, Quinta Grande
and Campanário. The road dives beneath Campanário's
church in a tunnel and soon describes a breathtaking arc out
over the coast on a long bridge. Then you enter the final,
long tunnel. Keep in the *left-hand* lane as you near the end
of it, to follow signposting for 'São Vicente' (17km). (The
right-hand lane is the turn-off to Ribeira Brava down on the
coast, 2km away.)

Just 15 minutes from Funchal you're on your way — this
first leg used to take a good hour and a half! After a straight
run along a narrow canyon graced with poplars, the road
begins its winding ascent. Beyond **Serra de Água** you pass
several picnic areas (⌂) and then the Pousada dos Vinháticos (▲ ⌂), beautifully sited below a ridge — the aptly-
named Crista de Galo ('Cock's Comb'). Some 2.5km further
uphill (past the Residencial Encumeada ▲), Walk 4 comes
in along a track on the right. The snaking ascent ends at **Encu-
meada★**, just at the centre of the island (1004m/3293ft;
28km ✗). Park on the left at the far side of this pass (⌂),
from where there are spectacular views down to the north
coast and up to the Paúl da Serra in the west and the high
peaks to the east. Walk 31 can begin here; Walk 20 ends on
the other side of the road. While you are here, *do* take the
opportunity to see the great Levada do Norte, described on
pages 117-118 (Walk 32 and **P**32); the steps are on the south
side of the pass, opposite the bar/restaurant.

Then descend into São Vicente's welcoming valley
(⌂), past **Chão dos Louros**, a lovely laurel grove (⌂ with

18

Car tours 1 and 5, Walk 29: The graceful clock tower of Nossa Senhora de Fátima graces a hilltop in São Vicente's valley.

fireplaces). Soon you'll have good views (📷🎍) over Rosário's church and stream: in high summer the hayricks weave ribbons of gold into the tapestry of this emerald landscape. Beyond **Rosário** you find yourself in the settings shown above and on page 1. At **Feiteiras** you pass the ER208 to 'Ginjas' and 'Lanço'. Walk 29 begins and ends 3.1km up this road, at Miradouro. Beyond Miradouro, the road is still under construction to Estanquinhos on the Paúl da Serra.

Come into **São Vicente** (39km ✝🏔✕🍽⊕; photograph page 31), a good place to take a break for morning coffee … and to make a decision: are you going to try to fit in a detour to Porto Moniz? If it's now later than 10.00, you really don't have the time. If you *do* have time, use the notes for Car tour 5 on page 30 to go at least *part* of the way — to see the waterfalls west of Seixal.

On leaving São Vicente, look out for the chapel (✝) built into a hollowed-out rock south of the bridge. Then either turn left towards Seixal or follow the main tour: turn right on the coastal ER101 (🏔✕). After passing through a tunnel, your attention will be drawn to the chequered pattern made by the heath tree hedges protecting the terraces from the fierce northerly winds. Most of the fields are planted with vines, but this is for table wine; the vines which yield the grapes for the fine Madeira wines are grown in the south, around Estreito de Câmara de Lobos. The road takes you in shadow below menacing cliffs, before you skirt above the lava-fertile promontory of **Ponta Delgada** (46km ✕🍽) and soar up to a viewpoint (📷🎍) over the village setting and headlands to the east.

Above Ponta Delgada, a short stretch of cobbled road and an old, narrow tunnel are a delightful reminder of bygone

19

days, when driving round the island was a spine-rattling experience. Then the road turns inland, leaving the awesome coast for the green-gold gentleness of the great **Boaventura** (49km ▲▲✕⊕☰) valley. Walk 27, one of our all-time favourites, begins at the village church. Just past Boaventura there is a good viewpoint (☞) on the left. At the head of the valley (🖳) a road is being built to Curral das Freiras, via Falca.

The bucolic pleasures of this valley are a foretaste of the whole unforgettable landscape between Boaventura and Santana. Back on asphalt, pass above **Arco de São Jorge** (56km ⊕), decked out with vines and hedgerows and rainbows of flowers. The hillsides are cultivated almost down to the sea, along the sweeping curve *(arco)* of the bay. Climb past mossy cliffs and dark pines brightened by banks of agapanthus, to another *miradouro* (☞☰) with fine views back to Ponta Delgada, with its seaside church and swimming pool. Adjacent to this viewpoint are the Cabanas rondavels (▲▲✕).

Soon turn left for 'Vigia'. You pass roads left to the *vigia* ('lookout'; ☞) and lighthouse (☞), before coming into **São Jorge** (67km ✝🖳⊕). The richest baroque church outside Funchal is on your right. Walk 18, which descends the stupendous trail shown on page 29, can end here. Turn left on rejoining the ER101: beyond a bridge, you pass a road up right to Ilha, where Walk 28 ends.

Soon you come upon enticing views of **Santana★** (75km ▲▲✕🖳⊕), where orchards and market gardens roll down to the sea. If you haven't brought a picnic, this is the best place to stop for lunch. From Santana the tour travels via the ER101 to **Faial** and then the ER103 as far as Poiso; use the notes on pages 28 and 29 (Car tour 4). It's about two hours from Santana to Funchal and, hopefully, you will have time to walk to Balcões from **Ribeiro Frio** (Short walk 25) and drive to Arieiro from Poiso.

Past **Poiso** (100km *excluding* the detour to Arieiro), continue south to **Monte★** (108km ✝✿✕). The new cable car linking Monte with Funchal (opening in 2000) will ensure this village regains the fame it enjoyed in the 19th century! Walk above the delightful gardens to the church of Our Lady of the Mount, where you can see the tiny poignant statue to Madeira's patron saint. From the bottom of the church steps (departure point for the famous toboggan rides), you could follow the agapanthus-banked lane to the left (past the Monte Palace Gardens ✿), to Babosas Balcony (15 minutes return on foot). Here a baroque chapel looks out over the impressive bowl of Curral dos Romeiros in the João Gomes River valley. Walk 7 can begin here.

Now it's just 5km back to Funchal (113km).

2 EASTERN MADEIRA'S GENTLE CHARMS

Funchal • Palheiro Gardens • Camacha • Santo da Serra • Machico • Ponta de São Lourenço • Pico do Facho • Santa Cruz • Funchal

85km/53mi; 4 hours' driving; Exit A from Funchal (plan page 11)

On route: ☐ at São Lourenço Point, Santa Cruz; Picnics (see **P** symbol and pages 12-16): (7a-b), 8, (10), 11, 13; Walks 7-14

Roads are asphalted, but sometimes potholed. Allow a full day, to make the most of the Palheiro Gardens (open 09.30 to 12.30 except weekends/holidays) and São Lourenço Point.

L eave Funchal from Exit A (Rua Dr Manuel Pestana Júnior). Keep following 'Camacha'. Ignore two turnings right to São Gonçalo and a sign for 'Palheiro Golf'. Just past a fairly large electricity sub-station on your right, turn right (signposted 'Quinta do Palheiro'). The drive to the **Palheiro**

Levada da Serra (Picnic 10 and Walk 10)

Gardens★ (5km ✿) is shaded by planes and lined with lilies and camellias. Below the house, gentle terraces yield up ever-changing vistas of the formal and informal gardens, pools and fountains, avenues and parks surrounding the Count of Carvalhal's original *quinta* (▲▲) and chapel.

Return to the main road (ER102) and turn right, crossing the Levada dos Tornos (Walk 7). Now the road runs below the Levada da Serra (Walk 10), which may be joined at various points. Continue (✕🍽) up to **Camacha**★ (10km ▲▲✕🍽⊕WC), the centre of Madeira's willowcraft industry. The village square, the Achada da Camacha, overlooks the magnificent Porto Novo Valley. Short walk 7-3 and Walk 8 both begin here in the square.

Passing market gardens, continue to the wooded heights of **Eira de Fora** (🍽). There is a view down right over the Levada dos Tornos, before you come to **Águas Mansas** (15km) and pass the junction of the ER206 south (*P*7a-b; photograph page 66). Access to Short walk 10-3 is via the track on your left, 100m past this turn-off. Then round a bend to enter the great Boaventura basin, another valley irrigated by the Tornos. At 19km pass the ER202 left to Poiso; our favourite stretch of the Levada da Serra begins not far up this road (*P*10; photograph page 21) and would take you to Portela (Short walk 10-4, followed by Short walk 10-5).

At 21km fork right on the ER212 into **Santo da Serra** (22km ✿▲▲✕🍽), a wooded village with several fine *quintas*. Walk 9 starts here; Walk 10 could begin or end here. Beyond the church, ignore the first sharp left turn (by the hotel), but bear left at the Y-fork in front of the Quinta da Paz, to skirt the golf course. Bear left again beyond the clubhouse and continue down into Machico's valley, in 0.6km passing a right turn to the Capela dos Cardais, where Walk 9 can also start. Two viewpoints (📷) on this road afford superb perspectives on the flawless setting of emerald-green Machico Bay, Pico do Facho, and the sun-baked arm of São Lourenço Point.

From the second viewpoint, continue down to the ER101 and go left for **Machico**★ (30km ✝▲▲✕🍽⊕), Madeira's first settlement. Of particular interest are the Manueline church and the Chapel of Miracles. The latter, on the east side of the river, was founded in 1420 on the site of Zarco's first landfall; destroyed by a flood in 1803, the chapel was rebuilt later in the 19th century.

Leave Machico the way you came in and, at the petrol station, turn right for Portela. But then turn right again on the ER109 for Caniçal. (*Note:* If you are taking walkers to the start of Walk 11, watch for the signposted turn-off left to Maroços, only 100m after you join the Caniçal road. The walk starts exactly 4.3km from this turn-off.) Climbing the

There are superb views over the Bay of Funchal from Pináculo, an aloe-spiked promontory above São Gonçalo. What a stupendous view of the fireworks the nearby hotel must have on New Year's Eve!

lush eastern flanks of Machico's valley (✕), you come to the Caniçal tunnel (**P**11), where Walk 11 ends; Walks 12 and 14 and Short walk 11 begin here. Beyond a pretty line of palm trees fanning out above the grassy slopes, turn down right into **Caniçal** (38km ✕ and whaling **M**), a once-poor fishing port now bursting its seams with new buildings as a result of the adjacent tax-free industrial zone.

From here return to the main road and continue straight out (▲▲ ✕) to **São Lourenço Point★**. Use the notes on pages 76-78 to explore; perhaps picnic at Abra Bay (44km ⟨⟨◎⟩⟩ ⟨⟨⟨⟩⟩ **P**13; Walk 13) or one of the viewpoints (⟨⟨◎⟩⟩ ⟨⟨⟨⟩⟩).

On your return from the point, take the road just west of the tunnel to **Pico do Facho** (53km ⟨⟨◎⟩⟩), to admire the view over Machico and its bay, nestling below the hills of Santo da Serra. Continuing west (✕), pass the airport and, just beyond the ER207 north to Santo da Serra, turn left into delightful **Santa Cruz★** (64km ✝▲✕⊕). Here you can stretch your legs in the *til*-shaded square and visit the bright-white church of São Salvador, one of the finest Manueline buildings on the island and the largest church outside Funchal. The lido, with its cafés, palms and pebble beach, is a pleasant place to relax.

Bridges soon span the great clefts of the Boaventura (🚆) and Porto Novo valleys. Short walk 8 begins at **Assomada**'s church (**P**8). Just beyond the ER205 up right to Camacha, turn left down to **Caniço** (75km ✝▲✕🚆⊕), a major tourist centre. After visiting the church, head back north to the ER204, quickly coming to **Cançela** (78km ✕🚆). *Carefully follow signposting for São Gonçalo,* keeping in the left-hand lane in order to join the narrow old road hugging the coast. Some 2km along, pull over left at the viewpoint shown above (⟨⟨◎⟩⟩). Then take advantage of the inevitable traffic jam in **São Gonçalo** (✕🚆) to admire the fine old houses on the eastern outskirts of Funchal, before regaining the centre (85km).

3 THE CORRAL AND THE CAPE

Funchal • Pico dos Barcelos • Eira do Serrado • Curral das Freiras • Câmara de Lobos • Cabo Girão • Funchal

64km/40mi; 3 hours' driving; Exit B from Funchal (plan page 10)

On route: ⍋ on the ER107 to Curral, Cabo Girão; Picnic (see *P* symbol and pages 12-16): 3; Walks 3, (4), 6. (Picnic 1 and Walk 1 are near this tour, but are best reached direct from Funchal by bus.)

For the best light, do this short tour in the afternoon. The road between Funchal and Cabo Girão is heavily congested. The ER107 to Curral das Freiras, although steep and winding, is well built-up at the sides.

Either take the 'P. de Barcelos' exit off the Via Rápida or leave Funchal by Exit B (the statue to Freedom in front of Reids Gardens, signposted 'Estádio'). Leaving from Exit B, you very soon pick up signposting for Pico dos Barcelos. As you approach the slender spire of São Martinho's church, on a hill, turn right, cross the expressway, and continue to **Pico dos Barcelos★** (6km ✕☻WC), a tree-shaded *miradouro* offering fine views over Funchal and the east.

Continue north, now following signposting to the Eira do Serrado. The ER107 climbs through forests of eucalyptus and pine splintered by golden sun-shafts (✕⍋). A good viewpoint (☻) over the Socorridos ravine is passed on the left, before you reach the right-hand fork to the **Eira do Serrado★** (18km ☻WC*P*3; ▲▲ under construction). No doubt you will join the crowds and climb the paved path to the main viewpoint, from where there are stupendous views over Curral, 400m/ 1300ft below. But to hug all this splendour to yourself, follow Walk 3 from the 15min-point (page 47) for five to ten minutes. Better still, do *all* of Walk 3, then take a bus back to your car!

Beyond the Eira the road winds down and through two tunnels into the crater-like ravine where **Curral das Freiras★** (the 'Nuns' Corral'; 22km ✕WC; photograph pages 46-47) huddles below awesome heights. Walk 3 ends not far below the village. The ER107 is being built from here to Boaventura.

Return the same way and, 1km past Pico dos Barcelos (just before São Martinho Church), turn right, to get on the expressway west. After crossing the Socorridos, take the exit for **Câmara de Lobos★** (✕⊕ and ✝ founded by Zarco in 1424). Follow the one-way system down to the bandstand and park. When you've looked at the colourful fishing boats and the church, leave on the tarred road signposted 'CTT

The Quinta do Jardim da Serra ('Garden in the Mountains') can be reached by taking a detour from Estreito de Câmara de Lobos.

From the top of Cabo Girão, safe behind iron railings, you can marvel at the toy ships at sea some 580m/1900ft below you ... and at the tenacity of the sure-footed Madeiran farmers working their tiny terraces.

Correos'. As you make the sharp left turn back to the main road (🚌), a plaque above a terrace on the right alerts you to the place where Sir Winston Churchill painted the curving white arc of the village against the backdrop of the awesome red cape, Cabo Girão. Continuing west on the old road (ER229; 🚌), turn right just over 1.5km uphill, to climb to **Pico da Torre** (🕶), a lovely viewpoint over Câmara de Lobos.

The ER229 winds below **Estreito de Câmara de Lobos** (44km ✕ ⊕).* The island's best grapes are grown around here, and an exceptionally gorgeous display of terraced vineyards pours down the hillsides below **Garachico**'s church (photograph page 57). The road crosses the Levada do Norte at **Quinta Grande**; Short walk 6-2 begins here. Just 0.8km further on, turn left to **Cabo Girão★** (51km ✕ ⼌ 🕶WC). From this sea-cliff you enjoy the spectacular view over Funchal's bay shown above. But if you are a keen walker, your eyes will be drawn to the 'winged' bridge over the Socorridos and then up the valley to the mountains.

From here return to Funchal on the expressway (64km).

*If you have time for a detour (either 8.5 or 14km return), turn right into Estreito, curl left round the church, then drive straight uphill. Just beyond a chapel on the left (0.7km past the church), you cross the Levada do Norte (Walk 6). At a fork (1.6km) keep left for 'Foro' and 'Jardim da Serra'. Ignore a road on the right (3.4km) and curve round left over a bridge. Almost immediately, bear right at a Y-fork (keeping the 'Central da Pereira' on your left). You will come to the lovely *quinta* shown opposite (4.2km), built in the 1800s by the English consul, Henry Veitch. From here he sent fruit, books and old wines to Napoleon, when the Northumberland laid anchor in Funchal on its passage to St Helena. From here you can continue uphill for another 2.5km to the end of the road: Boca da Corrida, the superb viewpoint where Walk 4 begins.

4 MOUNTAINS AND MORE MOUNTAINS!

Funchal • Poiso • Pico do Arieiro • Portela • Porto da Cruz • Achada do Teixeira • Santana • (São Jorge • Arco de São Jorge) • Faial • Ribeiro Frio • Funchal

*141km/88mi; about 6-7 hours' driving, **excluding** the detour to Arco de São Jorge; Exit A from Funchal (plan page 11)*

On route: ⋔ at Poiso, Pico do Arieiro, ER202 west of the Levada da Serra, ER108 north of Portela, ER103 around Ribeiro Frio, Pico das Pedras, ER218 to Achada do Teixeira, path to Pico Ruivo, Queimadas Park; Picnics (see *P* symbol and pages 12-16): 2, 10, 15, 16, 19, 20, (22), 25; Walks: 2, 7, 9, 10, 14-21, (22-24), 25, 26, (28)

*It is usual to include the mountainous northeast of the island in what is often called a 'Santana Tour', covering all of central Madeira (our Car tour 1). We find this very hectic and urge you to devote an entire day to visiting the great rugged peaks and the gentle moorland roads radiating from Poiso Pass. This tour fits in nicely with Car tours 5 or 6, providing a leisurely two-day introduction to many of Madeira's best landscapes. Start out early in the morning and **aim to reach Arieiro no later than 09.30**; clouds often descend by about 10.00. If you do not plan to take any short walks, you will have time to go further west than Santana — to São Jorge (18km return; 1h) or possibly Arco (38km return; 2h) — a part of the island not to be missed. Although this tour is long, the roads are all good, although winding and occasionally potholed.*

The direct route to Arieiro from Funchal is Exit C (Rua 31 de Janeiro; ER103), via Monte. But we suggest you try another way: take Exit A and use the notes on page 21 past the entrance to the **Palheiro Gardens★** (5km). In a minute more, the ER201 joins from the left. Turn up left here and follow this pine- and eucalyptus-shaded road northwest. You cross the Levada dos Tornos (Walk 7) and pass the cobbled trail where Walk 10 begins. At **Terreiro da Luta★** (14km ✝✗☞WC) a statue to Our Lady of Peace commemorates the sufferings of the people of Funchal during World War I. At the base of the statue there is a rosary made from the anchor chains of ships torpedoed in Funchal harbour. In the early 1900s a luxurious cog railway climbed up here via Monte. The views over the city's setting are superb, but soon you must press on! Join the ER103 ahead and turn right.* The smooth asphalt road, lined with hydrangeas and agapanthus, snakes its way up past the Montado do Pereiro (Δ) to a barren plateau and then **Poiso Pass** (1400m/4600ft; 20km ✗⋔☞).

Here turn left on the highland road (ER202) to **Pico do Arieiro★** (1818m/5963ft; 27km ▲✗☞⋔WC*P*19; Walk

*Some 3km beyond Terreiro da Luta, at the Montado do Barreiro forestry house, you will pass two roads on the left. The first goes to a viewpoint at Pico Alto (⋔) and the second (open daily from 08.00 to 19.00) climbs all the way to the Pico do Arieiro road. While most maps indicate a through road, you *cannot* get to Arieiro this way (there is a cul-de-sac sign at the entrance). A locked gate, installed to prevent vandalism to plant life, bars access to the ER202, where there is no guards' house. But *do* explore this beautiful forestry road (⋔) when you have the time.

19; photograph pages 90-91). Visit too the **Miradouro do Juncal** (☞ 15min return; the path begins almost opposite the *pousada*): from here you have fine views over the sweep of the Metade Valley down to Faial and Penha de Águia ('Eagle Rock'). Later in the day, you will have another 'eagle's eye' view of the Metade, from Balcões.

On your return, watch for the ice house hidden below the road on your right, some 2km below the peak ('Poço da Neve'; **P**2; photograph page 13). Walk 2 starts here. Then pass the meteorological station and come again to Poiso (34km). Now go straight ahead on the ER202 opposite, a beautiful moorland road. After 4.2km you could park for Walk 26 (photograph page 108). Overlooking the reservoir at Santo da Serra, you descend past shaded 🌲 and then cross the Levada da Serra (**P**10; photograph page 21). You meet the ER102 at the Sítio das Quatro Estradas ('place where four roads join'; 42km); Walk 9 and Short walk 10-3 end here; Short walk 10-4 begins here. Turn left, passing the ER212 into Santo da Serra (🚌) and continuing north to **Portela★** (49km ✗☞**P**15), where Walk 25 ends and Walk 15 begins. Here you enjoy the superb view to the north coast shown on pages 82-83, with Penha de Águia dominating the landscape.

From Portela take the ER108 north (☞🌲). Alternative walk 16, through a valley called 'Watch you don't fall!', begins at **Referta** (52.5km). Curl down into bright **Porto da Cruz** (55km ✗🚌⊕), where Walks 14 and 15 end. Pass a good viewpoint (☞) back over the village as you climb west to skirt the towering mass of Eagle Rock. Don't blink, or you might miss **Cruz** (57km; **P**16), where Walk 16 begins and the descent from Eagle Rock ends (Walk 17). Just before crossing the bridge over the Ribeira de São Roque, turn right (signposted '**Penha de Águia**'). Walk 17 begins 1.1km uphill, at the Bar Galé. Continue to a turning circle at the end of the road, from where there is a fine view (☞) towards Faial and the high peaks. Return, cross the bridge (☞) and pass the ER103 on your left (60km ✗). Skirt the centre of **Faial** (✗⊕) and make for Santana, for the present ignoring the two roadside viewpoints. The sun is now too high for this landscape to be seen at its best.

With good planning you will reach the Santana area late in the morning. Before coming to the village centre, turn left on the ER218 for 'Pico das Pedras/Pico Ruivo'. Climb to the crossing of the Levada do Caldeirão Verde at the Rancho Pico das Pedras (▲▲✗). Walk 21 and Short walk 21 both begin here. Some 250m further uphill you come to the **Pico das Pedras** forestry house (✿🌲 with fireplaces). Beyond two well-sited viewpoints (☞🌲), one of them involving a stiff climb, the road ends on a plateau. This is the **Achada do**

Teixeira★ (79km 📷🌲), where Walk 19 ends and Walk 20 begins. You could picnic here (***P**20*) at Homem em Pé (photograph page 93) or on the Ruivo path (🌲). Or you might like to walk to Queimadas* (🌲✿*P*22); if so, park by the Rancho Pico das Pedras.

Turn back to **Santana★** (93km ▲▲✕🍴⊕), where Walk 18 begins and Walk 22 ends. The village is an enchantment of patchwork-quilt gardens and orchards set below spectacular mountains. Break for lunch here, if you didn't bring a picnic. Then decide whether to press on to São Jorge (♣🍴⊕📷) or Arco (📷🌲✕), returning the same way. You want to be leaving Santana at about 15.00.

Return to Faial. It's now afternoon, and you are just in time to enjoy the best views from the two *miradouros* (📷) west of the village. Clouds scud across the sky, creating fascinating mosaics of light and shade on this dramatic landscape. Eagle Rock is seen from base to summit, standing guard over church and village, at the confluence of three great river valleys: the Metade, the Seca and the São Roque. This superb panorama is likely to be one of your most lasting impressions of Madeira.

Beyond **Faial** turn right on the ER103 (✕). Look left to see São Roque atop its *lombo* (the spine separating the parallel ravines of the São Roque and Metade rivers), as you follow the road up the spectacularly-terraced Seca Valley towards the mountains shown in silhouette on pages 84-85. Walk 21 ends at **Cruzinhas** (105km), in a magnificent splurge of cultivation (photograph page 96).

Just after you cross the Metade, pass a rough road right to the power station at Fajã da Nogueira (Walk 24). Climb past the fruit trees of **Cedro Gordo** and forests of cedar, cypress, pine and eucalyptus (🌲). Beyond a viewpoint (📷) left over the Ribeiro Frio Valley, you reach the sweet coolness of **Ribeiro Frio★** (111km ✕🌲✿). Take a break here to walk to the Balcões: see Short walk 25, page 104. From these 'Balconies' (📷*P*25) you have a view to contrast with that from the Juncal *miradouro* visited earlier in the day. Eagle Rock is seen again, presiding over the north coast villages. But from the Balcões the jagged central peaks dominate the scene. The Metade takes its source on these heights, and its tributaries feed the power station 250m/800ft below you (Walk 24), from where the Tornos Levada flows on to irrigate the southeast.

Beyond the trout hatcheries and small botanical garden,

---

*Some 1km west of the ER218, a very narrow, poorly-surfaced lane with few passing places climbs steeply to Queimadas (Walks 22, 23 and 28). It's usually easier to walk from the Rancho Pico das Pedras (30 minutes each way), unless you're lucky enough to find the road newly tarred.

wind uphill (⌂) through conifers, back to **Poiso** (118km).
There's one more moorland road to be explored: the ER203,
0.5km south of the pass, signposted left to Camacha. This
delightful route overlooks Gaula and the Desertas. When
you lose the moorland to gorse, ferns and pine, you cross the
Levada da Serra at Paradise Valley (Short walk 10-2). Half a
kilometre further on, meet the ER102 (✗) and turn right for
Funchal (141km).

*Driving east from São Jorge, you will admire this spectacular old trail
on the mountainside below Santana. Walk 18 descends it, then follows
a cliff-side path beside the crashing sea,
before climbing back up to São Jorge.*

5 PORTO MONIZ AND THE PAÚL DA SERRA

Funchal • São Vicente • Seixal • Porto Moniz • Ribeira da Janela Valley • Paúl da Serra • Bica da Cana • Encumeada • Funchal

126km/78mi; 5-6 hours' driving; take the expressway from Funchal.

On route: 🚏 at Vinháticos, Encumeada, Chão dos Louros, above Rosário, Porto Moniz, Fonte do Bispo, Rabaçal, Bica da Cana; Picnics (see **P** symbol and pages 12-16): 31-33, (35-37), 38, 39, (42); Walks: 20, (29), 31-34, (35-37), (42)

*This is the easiest tour to the west and combines especially well with Car tour 4, to provide a two-day programme covering almost all of Madeira's best landscapes. The southwestern part of the island is well worth exploring (see Car tour 6), but is a very long drive — especially for those based east of Funchal. You will have to go slowly on the narrow corniche road between São Vicente and Porto Moniz — where you may encounter tour coaches (but they usually ply this route in the afternoon, which is a good reason for you to be there in the **morning** — in addition to seeing the corniche in the best light). Watch out for potholes!*

Follow Car tour 1 to **São Vicente** (39km 🛆⌂🛆✕🖵⊕). North of the village, turn left on the corniche road to Porto Moniz: for 15 kilometres it soars up cliffs and swoops down again to the sea, racing in single-minded determination through tunnels and waterfalls. *Drive carefully; sound your horn at blind corners; lights on in the tunnels.* (The edge of the road is usually built up with solid concrete; motorists should not find it vertiginous.)

There are three viewpoints (📷) on the corniche; the first is at a tunnel 4.5km along. Some 2km further on you come to **Seixal** (47km 🛆✕⊕), where a graceful church looks out over the coast. Notice the terrifyingly-steep vineyards edged with feathery heath tree branches. If you haven't brought a picnic, there is a superb fish restaurant down by the sea

Santa's church decked out for a 'festa'. The arch and flagpoles are wrapped in laurel leaves. Facing page: São Vicente and the nearby Levada da Fajã do Rodrigues (Walk 29).

(follow 'Cais'). The next viewpoint is at another tunnel, just after you pass *through* waterfalls. Here you look out east past Seixal, as far as São Jorge; in the foreground, the falls cascade over towering cliffs where Pride of Madeira clings tenaciously. West lies **Ribeira da Janela**: village and river take their name from the 'window' *(janela)* in the 'sea-horse' rock just off the coast. Just past the bridge is the final outlook (📷) over this dramatic coastal landscape. Soon you're in **Porto Moniz★** (56km 🏨△✗🛒⊕🎋). Its restaurants are popular with coach parties, but you can picnic on the coastal lava rocks or swim in the maze of glassy sea water pools.

Climb out of Porto Moniz on steep hairpin bends, past two bird's-eye viewpoints (📷) over the village setting. Just 3.5km up from the roundabout by the petrol station, you pass the road off left to Walk 42 (**P**42), signposted to Lamaceiros. Beyond **Santa** (photograph opposite), at the cattle market (62km), turn left on the ER110 and follow it southeast along Madeira's greatest ravine. The far-off views over the north and south coasts are splendid. But even more impressive is the size and magnificence of the **Janela Valley**. Virgin forests of heath and laurel cloak the mountainsides like green sable.

Our first stop is at the ruined 'Casa do Elias' at **Quebra-das** (67km 📷), from where there is a superb view over Ribeira da Janela on its conical hilltop. Soon come to another *mira-douro* near **Fonte do Bispo** (73km 📷🎋), from where the ER210 runs south down to Prazeres. If you have binoculars, looking southeast you can see the Rabaçal houses at the head of the valley … and even the Risco waterfall. Across the valley, on a hill, the curiously bare area studded with trees is the idyllic Fanal, where some of the island's oldest laurels are still to be found (Walk 34; photograph page 8). Beyond the Fanal, the peaks in the east rise above cloud necklaces. The lighthouse at Ponta do Pargo is glimpsed in the west.

At 80km, past the ER211 south to Calheta (Alternative

walk 37-1), you reach the head of the valley, by a reservoir and parking bay (☞*P*38 and Walk 38; photograph page 131). Here you are just above Rabaçal, a beauty spot much beloved by Madeirans. A detour down the ***very narrow*** road would add 4km to the tour (🚹*P*37a-e; Walk 37).

Past the Pico da Urze (⛰) you are on the **Paúl da Serra**, so very different from the Janela Valley. Even in winter rain the Paúl has a strange beauty: the moors take on a golden hue, the bracken throws up wine-red flames, and seagulls swirl over the marshes. On sunny days, the air is bright as diamonds. Beyond the signpost left 'Fanal/Ribeira da Janela' (Walk 34), you come to the ER209 south: Walks 35 and 36 begin 4km down this road (*P*35, 36). Turn left for Bica da Cana, passing a statue to Nossa Senhora da Serra on the right. Walk 39 (photographs pages 34 and 132) begins at the signpost left to 'Estanquinhos' (*P*39). But keep *right* here for **Bica da Cana**: two concrete pillars mark the stone-laid trail to this old hunting lodge, on your left (88.5km 🚹 and ☞ at the end of the track above the house; *P*33 and Walk 33).

Continue on the ER110 for the breathtaking descent to Encumeada. You look out to the great peaks in the east, the landscape shown on page 119. Some 4.5km from Bica, a signpost on the right, 'Lombo do Mouro', alerts you to the refuge shown on page 116 (*P*31 and Walk 31). Just over 1km further on, you pass a sign on the left with an orange stripe and a star; Alternative walk 33 begins its climb to Pináculo here. Soon you skirt above the magnificent Rabaças and Norte levadas, and you follow them to **Encumeada** (98km ☞🚹✕). From here retrace your outgoing route to Funchal (126km).

Paúl da Serra

6 THE SUNNY SOUTHWEST COAST

Funchal • Ribeira Brava • Canhas • Arco da Calheta • Prazeres • (Paúl do Mar) • Ponta do Pargo • Ribeira da Janela Valley • Bica da Cana • Encumeada • Funchal

*163km/101mi; 7-8 hours' driving **without detours**; Exit D from Funchal (plan page 10)*

On route: 🍴 at Campanário, Ponta do Sol, Arco da Calheta, Prazeres, east of Raposeira, north of Ponta do Pargo, Fonte do Bispo, Rabaçal, Bica da Cana, Encumeada, Vinháticos; Picnics (see **P** symbol and pages 12-16): (6), 31, 33, (35-37), 38, 39, (40); Walks (5), 6, 20, 30-35, (36, 37), 38, 39, (40), 41

This tour follows inland roads all the way west — for the views and the walks. If you find endless sorties into and out of valleys irksome, take the expressway to Ribeira Brava and then the coastal road to Calheta. If you have already done Car tour 5, vary your return: take the ER211 from the Paúl to down to Calheta, then follow the coast and expressway.

Leave Funchal by Exit D, passing the Lido. Beyond Câmara de Lobos, the road winds below **Estreito de Câmara de Lobos** (44km ✕⊕; Walk 6) and **Garachico**. The road crosses the Levada do Norte at **Quinta Grande** (Short walk 6-2) just 0.8km before the left turn to **Cabo Girão★** (Car tour 3). About 5km beyond **Campanário** (✕🍴⊕🍴), at the KM172 marker, you pass a road on the right signposted to 'S João' and 'S Paulo'. It leads to Boa Morte (**P**6) and Fontes (Walk 5). Soon you're circling steeply down into **Ribeira Brava** (31km ▲✕🍴⊕M and ✝ founded in the 1500s). Bright umbrellas cheer the esplanade, where Walks 30 and 31 end. The Museu Etnológico, portraying the development of the island through the ages, is well worth a visit.

Turn right inland off the esplanade (signposted to Porto Moniz) and then immediately turn left over the bridge, to climb the ER222. After about 8km Lombada da Ponta do Sol (✝) is signposted up to the right; a detour to the village would take you to the beautiful old manor *(solar)* visited on Walk 30. The road (🚗🍴) soon passes above Ponta do Sol; it's worth a 1km detour down left into the village for morning coffee (✕🍴⊕🍴 and ✝ founded in the 15th century).

Just beyond the church in **Canhas** (43km ✝✕) notice the first of the 14 Stations of the Cross on your right; after the last, on a straight stretch of road (🍴), there is a monument to St Theresa (✝). Nearby is the taxi rank (if you are dropping off passengers for Walks 34-37). Not far along, the ER209 heads up right to the Paúl da Serra. Soon you come to two dramatic viewpoints (🚗🍴) straight down over the sparkling houses and banana trees of Madalena do Mar, 450m/1500ft below (photograph overleaf).

Interesting churches, where some artefacts remain from the days of their founding, are to be found at the three Calhetas. The first is the Manueline **Loreto** chapel (✝), where Walk 35 ends: it is on the left, on the western outskirts of

Top: 'Esmeraldo's domain', near Lombada da Ponta do Sol (Walk 30); middle: bird's-eye view over Madalena do Mar; bottom: Pico Ruivo do Paúl, from the Estanquinhos/Bica da Cana junction (Walk and Picnic 39)

Arco da Calheta — not far past a road up right to another splendid viewpoint over Madalena do Mar on Pico do Arco (📷✗). The next is the 15th-century mother church in Calheta (♠🏠✗🚇⊕), 3km south of the ER222. The third is the 16th-century Reis Magos Chapel at **Estreito da Calheta** (♠✗), also below the road.

Climb under mimosa to **Prazeres** (67km 🏠🚻), where Walk 40 begins. A detour left to the hotel would take you to a splendid viewpoint over Paúl do Mar, 600m/2000ft below (📷*P*40; photograph page 15). Walk 41, along the photogenic levada shown on page 135, starts just below the church at **Raposeira**. Soon you pass the turn-off left to Paúl do Mar (ER223 via Fajã da Ovelha, at 72km; 🚻). If you have time, this 16km return detour is spectacular, and you will see some fine basalt chimneys in the rock before you reach the village, where Walk 40 ends.

The main tour bypasses these viewpoints, to make for **Ponta do Pargo** (81km ✗). Following 'Farol', turn left off the main road, then go right. A final left turn takes you to the lighthouse★ (83km 🏠📷), the most westerly point on Madeira.

Return to the ER101 and head north (🚻✗) for some 14km to the ER110, then turn right for 'Funchal'. Use the notes on page 31 from the 62km-point (Car tour 5) to continue, and return to town via the expressway (163km).

34

❀ Walking

Some 100 long and short walks are described in this Sixth edition, but you can devise many more for yourself, covering the length and breadth of the island. Most of our walks are linear because they follow old trails and the levadas. If you have hired a car, don't be discouraged by the lack of circular walks. *Take the time to plan ahead: study the maps and the bus timetables.* You can use your car and the buses (or taxis) in tandem. Remember that all the walks are keyed into the car tours, and the best access routes and parking details are given where relevant.

Beginners: Many walks are suitable for you. Start with those described as easy, and be sure to check all the short and alternative walks — some are easy versions of the longer walks. Look, too, at the picnic suggestions.

Experienced walkers: If you are accustomed to rough terrain and have a head for heights, you should be able to take most of the walks in this book in your stride. Provided, of course, that storm damage or bulldozing has not made the way unsafe, and *provided that you follow the route as we describe it.* If you have not reached one of our landmarks after a reasonable time, you must go back to the last 'sure' point and start again.

Experts: You should manage all the walks easily, *provided that you are used to very sheer unprotected drops* (some levada paths give virtually no respite from constant 'exposure'). We've also alerted you to some other walks you might like to tackle.

It is important that *all* walkers, whether beginners or experts, read and *heed* the Country code on page 8.

Guides, waymarking, maps

Quite a few of our routes edge sheer drops and are potentially dangerous; under 'Grade' we say that you must be sure-footed and have a head for heights. Until you get used to Madeira's terrain and know your 'vertigo tolerance', why not try one of these walks with a **guided group**? Several firms now operate inexpensive minibus tours with guides throughout the year; enquire at the Tourist Office.

During the late 1990s several routes were **signposted** and a few even **waymarked** with red and yellow flashes (two horizontal stripes mean *continue this way;* X means *do not go this way*). We will refer to these waymarks where they existed at time of writing.

	no danger
	some danger
	very dangerous!
★	flat or slight ascent/descent
★★	moderate ascents/descents
★★★	very strenuous
	Example: no danger, but
★★	some effort required

You will also come upon simple star- and colour-coded signs erected by the Regional Forestry Commission for the benefit of Madeirans who like to walk. The colour refers to the potential danger and the stars to the effort required. *We do not always agree with their gradings!*

Our walking **maps** have been completely redrawn for this edition, based on the latest 1:50,000 two-sheet map of the island published in 1995 by the Instituto Geográfico e Cadastral* and notes we have drawn up in the field. We have enlarged our maps to a scale of 1:40,000 to include a bit more detail, but the only paths shown on our maps are those we knew to be viable *at time of writing*, even if they were no longer routes described in the book. (For example, we show the footpath from Boca dos Namorados to Curral das Freiras, although we have omitted that 'classic' walk from this edition because we feel the footpath itself is now too short.) *Note that some of the paths we show are very difficult or vertiginous; unless you are an expert, please stick to the walks described (those marked in green or purple).*

Where to stay

If you have only a week on the island, or if walking is not your top priority, it's best to stay in **Funchal**. The bus network radiates from the capital. But the good news for keen walkers is that there is now *good hotel accommodation all over the island — in villages and in the mountains*, more frequent bus services, and more fly-drive packages than ever before. Judicious use of the bus timetables — together with a hired car, if you so choose — will take you to a good selection of walks *wherever* you are based.

Our walks pass by several 'rest houses' in Madeira's mountains. These are for the use of government officials, school parties, etc — not for foreign visitors (although you will be welcome to picnic in the grounds).

The only **camping sites** are at Porto Moniz and Montado do Pereiro. Check the web: www.madeira-camping.com.

*These maps should be available from your local map specialist. But be warned: they highlight *roads and tracks;* few paths are shown. Their current cost is more than the price of this book and, although they were designed for reproduction at a scale of 1:50,000, they are almost impossible to use 'on the ground', because paths and tracks are printed in pale grey.

Weather

Madeira has fine walking weather all year round, although summer is most reliable (and usually not too hot). Equinoctial rains can be expected in late September/October and in March/April, but there will be many fine days as well. June, when the island is often covered by a 'hood' of low-lying clouds (the *capacete*), is the only month best avoided.

Safe walking demands accurate reading of the weather signs and common sense. Outside summer many walks, especially in the north and west, can be treacherous. Even on the most glorious winter's day, levada paths will be full to overflowing and some mountain trails like waterfalls. *Never forget that anywhere on the island, at any time of year, a landslide can wipe out a path overnight.*

Apart from the seasons, Madeira's weather is determined by **wind direction**. Whatever the season, the weather will be at its best with a light northeasterly (trade) wind. If the wind swings round to west or (worst of all) southwest, unsettled weather follows. The central mountains catch up the clouds carried by these winds; read the signs to find the best 'microweather' for your walk:

- **Strong winds** from any direction except east, bring rain, if not storms. (Eg, if a strong northeasterly blows in, we head for the southwest.)
- **Strong wind from the east or south of east *(leste):*** This hot, dry wind from Africa guarantees good walking everywhere, with crystal clear views on the heights.
- **Mild winds from any direction except south or southwest** afford good walking all round the island.
- **Mild winds from the south/southwest** bring rain!
- As a rule of thumb, the **Desertas Islands** can serve as a 'ready-reckoner' for weather signs:

— If they are clearly visible (wind from W of N): the southeast, northeast and east are clear — at least in the valleys. The west is cloudy.

— If they are hazy or hardly visible (wind from the E, S, SE): the south may be cloudy, but walking is generally good everywhere.

— If they are cloudy (wind from the NE): the west, southwest and northwest are clear; eastern areas may be cloudy.

— If they seem very close and there is a white line on the horizon (wind from S, SW): rain is coming within 24 hours.

- The general pattern is a clear morning, with clouds gathering by mid-day, and the sky clearing again by mid-afternoon. *Early starts are recommended!*
- Telephone 150 for a recorded weather forecast (in Portuguese).

What to take

If you are already on Madeira and haven't walking boots or a torch or rucksack, you can still do many of our walks. But don't attempt the more difficult ones without proper equipment. For each walk in this book, we tell you the *minimum* equipment necessary. Where we require walking boots, there is *no substitute:* you will need to rely on the grip and ankle support they provide, as well as their waterproof qualities. For all other walks wear stout lace-up shoes with thick rubber or 'Vibram'-type soles, to provide good grip. Do *not* venture on walks requiring a torch unless you have one — some levada tunnels are exceedingly long, and you *must* be able to see both the roof (for possible projections) and the path, because the water in the channel may be very deep, cold, and fast-moving.

You may find the checklist below useful:

walking boots (which must be broken-in and comfortable)	anorak (zip opening)
	knives and openers
waterproof rain gear (outside summer months)	2 light cardigans
	bus timetables (see page 9)
plastic bottle and water purifying tablets	sunhat, suncream, sunglasses
	plastic rainhat
torch (with a wide beam)	extra pair of socks and bootlaces
walking stick	'Dog Dazer' (see 'Nuisances')
long-sleeved shirt (sun protection)	plastic groundsheet
long trousers, tight at the ankles	plastic plates, cups, etc
first-aid kit, including bandages	whistle, compass

Please bear in mind that we've not done *every* walk in this book under *all* weather conditions: we may not realise just how hot — or wet — some walks might be. Walking boots are *always* more useful than shoes, and we wear them all year round. In hot weather, *always* carry a long-sleeved shirt as well as your sunhat, and take your lunch in a shady spot. We rely on your good judgement to modify our equipment lists according to the season.

Nuisances

Dogs are not often a problem, but a 'Dog Dazer' is a good investment. For details about this ultrasonic dog deterrent contact Sunflower Books. There are *no* snakes, scorpions, poisonous spiders, or any other 'nasties' on the island.

Begging children have, frankly, become a menace. We *never,* under any circumstances, give them anything but a greeting. Obviously some walkers have given in to the blackmail, which has just aggravated the problem.

Large **groups of walkers** may cause your heart to sink, and they invariably stop for lunch at the places recommended in this book. If you know they are on your path, it's best to stop somewhere else to picnic.

Wait till your knees are accustomed to Madeira's terrain before tackling any steep descents, like the path to Ilha (left, Walk 28) or the old ice-runners' path down the Levada da Negra (right, Walk 2)

New roads have ruined many walks on the island. But now that the original frenzy of EU-subsidised road-building has calmed down, it is easier to appreciate many of the new roads — they've opened up the mountains to the less mobile tourists and are even speeding walkers to their chosen paths!

Portuguese for walkers

Once you venture off the beaten track, few of the older people speak English (the children often speak English or French). We have found an almost foolproof way to ask *and understand* directions in Portuguese. First, memorise the key questions and all their possible answers below; then **always phrase your questions so that you will get a yes ('seng') or no ('nowg') answer.**

KEY QUESTIONS (English/approximate Portuguese pronunciation)

'Please, sir (madam).   **Fahz** fah-**vohr**, sehn-**yohr** (sehn-**yoh**-rah).
Where is the levada to ...   **Ohn**-deh eh al leh-**vah**-dah **pah**-rah ...
  (the main road to …,   (ah ish-**trah**-dah **pah**-rah …,
  the footpath to …,   ah veh-**ray**-dah **pah**-rah …,
  the way to …,   oh cah-**mee**-noh **pah**-rah …,
  the bus stop)?   ah pah-**rah**-jeng)?
Many thanks.'   **Mween**-toh o-bree-**gah**-doh (a woman says: '**Mween**-toh o-bree-**gah**-<u>dah</u>).

POSSIBLE ANSWERS (English/approximate Portuguese pronunciation)

here/there	ah-**key**/ah-**lie**
straight ahead/behind	**semp**-reh eng **frengt**/ah-**trahs**
to the right/to the left	ah deh-**ray**-tah/ah ish-**kehr**-dah
above/below	eng **see**-mah/eng **bye**-joh

Ask a native speaker (your hotel porter, tour rep, or taxi driver) to help you with the pronunciation of these key phrases, as well as *place names.*

When you have your mini-speech memorised, always ask the many questions you can concoct from it in such a way that a yes/no answer will result. *Never* ask an open-ended question such as 'Where is the main road?' Even if you are standing on it, you probably won't understand the answer! Instead, ask the question and then **suggest the most likely answer yourself**, for example:

'**Fahz** fa-**vohr**, sehn-**yoh**-rah. **Ohn**-deh eh ah ish-**tra**-dah **pah**-rah Foon-

shal? Eh **sem**-preh eng **frengt**?' or '**Fahz** fa-**vohr**, sehn-**yor**. **Ohn**-deh eh ah Le-**vah**-dah dohs **Tor**-nohs? Eh eng **see**-mah ah deh-**ray**-tah?'

An inexpensive phrase book will help you compose other 'key' phrases and answers. It is always pleasant to greet people you meet on your walks with a 'good morning' or 'good afternoon' (bohm **dee**-ah, bo-ah **tard**).

Organisation of the walks

Our 42 main walks are grouped in three general areas: the southeast; the northeast and the great peaks; the west and northwest. We urge you to walk in *each* of these three areas, in order best to sample the island's varied landscapes.

We hope that the book is set out so that you can plan your walks easily — depending on how far you want to go, your abilities and equipment, the season … and what time you are willing to get up in the morning!

You might begin by looking at the fold-out touring map inside the back cover. Here you can see at a glance the overall terrain, the extent of the levada network, main and secondary roads, and the orientation of the walking maps in the text. Flipping through the book, you'll see that there is at least one photograph for each walk.

Having selected one or two potential excursions from the map and the photographs, turn to the relevant walk. At the top of the page you will find planning information: distance/time, grade, equipment, and how to get there. If the grade and equipment specifications are beyond your scope, don't despair! *We almost always suggest a short version of each walk* and, in most cases, these shorter walks are far less demanding of agility and equipment.

When you are on your walk, you will find that the text begins with an introduction to the overall landscape and then quickly turns to a detailed description of the route itself. Times are given for reaching certain key checkpoints. *Do compare your pace with ours on one or two short walks before tackling a long hike!* **Note that our times do not include any stops!** Allow extra time for picnics, photography, and any other breaks. Below is a key to the **symbols** on the walking maps.

═══	expressway	◦▸	source, tank, tap	♱	church
▬▬	main road	P	picnic suggestion (see pages 12-16)	⊕	cemetery
──	secondary road			†	shrine, statue
──	track, cobbled trail	🞕	best views	⊼	picnic site with tables
----	footpath, steps	⦂	danger! vertigo!		
6 →	main walk	🚌	bus stop	📖	map continuation
12 →	alternative walk	🚗	car parking	⼘	relay station
	levada, pipe	■	specific building	⚒	power station
2 →	levada walk	] [	tunnel	⚓	pylon
		—600	altitude (metres)	⚑	bar/shop

1 THE SOCORRIDOS VALLEY: LEVADA DOS PIORNAIS AND LEVADA DO CURRAL

Distance: 12.5km/7.8mi; 4h30min   **See also photograph page 7**

Note: There is now a stone-sorting works in the lower Socorridos Valley, which can be noisy. Try to save this walk for a Sunday.

Grade: moderate, but you must be sure-footed and agile. **Possibility of vertigo,** but railings protect most of the exposed sections. The second half of the walk involves a climb of 150m/500ft up to the Levada do Curral. *Little shade on the Levada dos Piornais.*

Equipment: stout shoes, sunhat, long-sleeved shirt, picnic, water

How to get there: *town* 🚌 45 to the first stop past the stadium (or on foot: see town plan on pages 10-11)
To return: town 🚌 16A from Pinheiro das Voltas

Shorter walks (equipment as main walk for both)

1 Stadium — Lombada. 7km/4.3mi; 2h10min. Grade as main walk (but no ascent); access as main walk. Follow the main walk to the viewpoint over the Socorridos, then return to the road passed at 1h45min and descend two minutes, to Lombada (the stop for *town* 🚌 1 or 3 is downhill from the bar, on the right). For even shorter walks, take *town* 🚌 4 to Amparo and join at the 30min-point, or *town* 🚌 2 to its terminus at Quebradas and join just after the 1h10min-point.

2 Levada do Curral. 7.5km/4.7mi; 2h. Grade as main walk (ascent of about 70m/230ft). Take *town* 🚌 16A and ask for 'Travessa do Pinheiro das Voltas'. Follow the main walk from the 2h30min-point to the end.

The magnificent Socorridos is the focal point for this walk. Just behind the noisy 'Ruhr Valley' river mouth, we are drawn into a magnificent tapestry of cultivation ... which eventually unravels at a spectacular gorge.

The bus drops you on the RUA DOS ESTADOS UNIDOS, just west of the STADIUM. **Start out** by walking back the way the bus came for about 30m/yds. Then descend steps on the right to the **Levada dos Piornais** and turn right along it. Dating from the 16th century, its water was not only used for irrigation: you will pass one of the millstones it turned (**10min**) and a few of the many old laundry basins. Within **15min** you can see the Lido, banana plantations ... and the eyesore of cranes and concrete in western Funchal. But soon you enjoy fine views of Cabo Girão and the terraces on its eastern flanks. Should you feel wary of the drops on the left, there is often room to walk on the right-hand side of the levada.

At **Amparo (30min)** three roads descend towards the coast. At the third road you must climb up a few paces to rejoin the levada (in front of an electricity sub-station). You are just south of SÃO MARTINHO CHURCH; its graceful spire is a familiar landmark. After a long cinderblock wall on the left, you come to a road (**1h**). Cross it to the electricity pylon opposite. Here steps take you back down to the levada, covered by a concrete walkway. In a minute, a cobbled road joins on the right. Follow it to a large house with decorative window tiles. At the left of the house steps take you back up to the levada.

Soon (under **1h10min**) the levada seems to end. Climb steps up to a road and turn right to a T-junction. Turn left and walk under the expressway, to another T-junction. Turn left again, immediately passing a supermarket (the terminus for *town* bus 2 is 30m/yds behind you). This is **Quebradas**. Walk past a turn-off left to the expressway and then the school, also on your left. Some 30m/yds past the school, cross the road and rejoin the levada. As you begin to round a small valley, the Socorridos bridge can be seen ahead. At **1h45min**, by an information panel about the Piornais Levada, note the road off left over the expressway: it descends to Lombada.

Now, suddenly, the levada turns north. The ground falls away, and you edge the breathtaking **Ribeira dos Socorridos**. Within the next 10 minutes, take a break by a grassy verge, to admire the 'winged' bridge and the valley's tapestry of green and gold plantations (**P**1). Sugar cane still persists along the muddy flats below in the river bed, and it's easy to imagine how nuns from the Santa Clara Convent fled to Curral under cover of cane in 1566. *(Shorter walk 1 turns back here.)*

Continuing along the levada, you will probably marvel at the golden curves of this watercourse hewn in the side of the rock ... sheer sculpture. Now you approach a series of short tunnels (no torch needed). Although the path through them is well protected, some people will find this stretch vertiginous. If you *do* go through the tunnels, you will have to stoop down *very* low, so take off your rucksack, or it will catch on the roof. Otherwise, just follow the green arrow and descend steps to a path which runs below the tunnels.

Whichever route you choose, you will come to a crossing of concrete steps, where you turn right uphill. When the steps run out (10 minutes above the Piornais Levada, by a house on the left), turn right on a path, following street lights. Join a road and continue ahead. At a Y-fork (where the left fork only goes to a garage), keep right downhill on cobbles, still following street lights. In under 15 minutes from the top of the steps (**2h30min**) you reach a junction at **Pinheiro das Voltas**. The bus stop for Funchal, to which you will return later, is ahead on the right. *(Shorter walk 2 joins here.)*

Turn *left* here, climbing a lane, the Travessa do Pinheiro das Voltas. The lane narrows; you pass a house and then greenhouses on the left. In eight minutes you reach the **Levada do Curral** at a T-junction with a road. Turn left here, passing house No 121 on the left, then following the levada past some pretty houses and gardens. After a brief diversion into the shady **Ribeira do Arvoredo**, you find yourself once again at the edge of the Socorridos.

When the houses end (**3h05min**), you will come to a red warning sign (see page 36). But continue ahead; railings pro-

Levada do Curral, near the pretty, isolated house (3h25min)

vide psychological comfort, and the route is not dangerous at this point. In under **3h25min** some well-tended vines spring up by a pretty, isolated house. Ignore a path down to the left 80 paces beyond it.* About 200m/yds past the house you will come to a gate. Unless there has been a landslide ahead, the gate should be open. But we suggest you *go only 100 paces beyond the gate,* to the first unprotected drops on the left. From this point you can see ahead a sheer escarpment, usually pouring with water and a jungle of vegetation. You have entered the gorge of the **Ribeira da Lapa** and will no doubt be as astonished as we were to find such an awesome place so close to Funchal. Ahead of you the aptly-named hamlet of Fajã ('landslip') sits abandoned on a hillside. Below you the Ribeira da Lapa flows into the Ribeira do Curral and the two become the Socorridos. When you consider that these rivers cut the valley and today feed four *major* levadas, you can perhaps imagine what a torrent the Socorridos was when some of Zarco's men very nearly drowned in it (the word *socorridos* means 'rescued men').

From here return the same way. When you get back to house 121 turn right, back down to **Pinheiro das Voltas**, and walk to the BUS SHELTER on the far side of the road (**4h30min**).

*This very steep and slippery path would take you down to the river bed at the confluence of the Lapa and Curral rivers — a highly recommended detour for energetic, agile walkers (allow 45min return and keep left at a fork partway down). Once down in the chasm, the source of the lower levada on the western side of the Socorridos lies not far to the left; the source of the Levada dos Piornais is just north of the Ribeira da Lapa.

2 FROM THE POÇO DA NEVE TO BARREIRA

Map begins on the reverse of the touring map and ends on page 43; photographs pages 6, 13 and 39 (right)

Distance: 7.5km/4.7mi; 3h15min

Grade: moderate-strenuous; a steep descent of 900m/2350ft. You must be sure-footed and have a head for heights (**danger of vertigo**).

Equipment: stout shoes (walking boots preferable), sunhat, picnic, water; cardigans, long trousers and anorak in cool weather

How to get there: 🚕 taxi to the Poço da Neve (ice house) on the ER202 2km below Pico do Arieiro, or 🚌 103 or 138 to Poiso (add 5km/3mi; 1h30min). The ice house is *below* the road, behind a walled lay-by. *To return: shuttle* 🚌 91 from Barreira to Trapiche, then connecting *town* 🚌 10A or 11

Shorter walk: Poço da Neve — sheep pens — Poço da Neve. 4.5km/ 2.8mi; 2h40min. Moderate; no danger of vertigo. Stout shoes, sunhat. Access/ return: 🚕 car or taxi to/from the Poço da Neve. Follow the main walk for 1h08min, then return the same way.

Alternative walk: Short walk 19 — Poço da Neve — Barreira. 11km/ 6.8mi; 4h45min. 🚕 taxi to Pico do Arieiro. Grade, equipment, return as main walk. Follow Short walk 19 (page 89) to the second viewpoint, then walk down the ER202 to the ice house to start this walk.

This thoroughly exhilarating walk has it all: glistening moorlands, a ribboning levada, and tremendous views. But wait till you've acquired your 'Madeira knees' — it's steep! So steep that it's unlikely any of the ice had a chance to melt back in the early 1900s, when men shouldering the precious commodity (wrapped in straw and packed in leather bags) fairly *ran* from the *poços da neve* ('snow pits') below Arieiro down to Funchal. The ice was not just served up in sorbets and drinks to the sybarites, it had important medical uses — to staunch bleeding, for example. Today only one ice house has been preserved and only one of the descent paths remains — the route we take down the Santo António Valley. (Another beautiful old stone-laid trail, on the east side of the Santa Luzia River, is completely broken away.)

Start out at the domed ICE HOUSE (**P**2) high on the eastern flanks of the **Ribeira de Santa Luzia**. Your route begins on the *western* side of the valley, where you can see a few paths running along the ridge. The easiest way to get there is to head *slightly left downhill* to the grove of squat heath trees shown at the left in the photograph on page 13. *Ignore* the track crossed a minute down (and if you encounter any signposts for 'Levada do Barreiro', *ignore them;* they do not lead to any route down to Funchal!). Once in the trees, you meet another crossing track. Turn right here and head *back up* the valley. In **30min** you encounter fencing: a gate, and then a stile, lead you to the point where you must cross the ravine — just above one of the concrete walls built into the river bed to calm the rush of water after heavy rain and prevent further erosion. On the far side of the river bed, turn

45

left and, about 15m/yds from the dam, watch for rocks on the right indicating the start of a clear earthen path. Follow this path up to a pass (**40min**), where you head right for about 10m/yds, to join the very narrow **Levada da Negra** (you cannot see the levada until you are almost upon it — be still for a moment and listen for the sound of its rushing water).

Turn left and let the levada guide you towards Funchal down a new valley — the **Ribeira de Santo António**. The city reveals itself in the V of the river valley. A rocky moonscape, with gnarled white heath tree limbs, alternates with ferny glens. Where the grassy pastureland is broken, luscious gold and russet volcanic hues emanate from the rock. On rounding a bend (**50min**), a picturesque spread of circular rock-built sheep pens appears on the right, stretching along a small plateau. Ten minutes later you can fork right across a shallow gully to visit the pens (**1h08min**), the setting for an annual shearing festival on 10th June.

Return to the levada. *(The Shorter walk heads back here.)* At **1h25min** you cross to the western side of the river. From now on the path is more eroded, and there are some vertiginous passages as the wild valley opens up below on the left. You'll have to be nimble, too, to negotiate a couple of awkward gullies. By **2h25min**, after you have passed below the trig point marking the summit of **Esteios**, there is a superb view down to the twin spires of Santo António's church; the single slender spire of São Martinho is silhouetted against the sea. Looking back up the valley, you can trace your route almost back to the sheep pens.

In just **2h35min** you pass through a gate and the steep descent ends, as you contour beneath a canopy of dense eucalyptus trees. In **2h40min**, two levadas shoot down to the left by a tiny waterhouse. Cross them and keep straight on, along this narrow and slippery red clay path. In **3h** you begin a new descent: turn left down a cobbled trail, with a rushing levada on either side. Soon enjoy another superb view — stretching from Boa Nova in the east to Cabo Girão in the west. Beyond a couple of isolated houses and a water tank on the left (**3h10min**), concrete comes underfoot. Three minutes later, at a Y-fork, keep *left* (the concrete lane ahead descends to Chamorra). In two minutes (**3h 15min**) you reach **Barreira** — just a tarred turning circle for SHUTTLE BUS 91.

3 FROM THE EIRA DO SERRADO TO CURRAL

Map on reverse of the touring map Distance: 2.5km/1.6mi; 1h20min
Grade: moderate descent of 500m/1650ft. In autumn and winter fallen chestnut leaves obscure the path, so watch your footing.
Equipment: stout shoes or walking boots, sunhat, water, optional picnic
How to get there: 🚗 to the Eira do Serrado viewpoint (Car tour 3) or 🚌 81 to the Eira turn-off on the ER107 (add 15min)
To return: 🚌 81 from the road *below* Curral village — back to Funchal, or to the Eira turn-off, to collect your car (add 15min)
Alternative walk: Eira do Serrado — Levada do Curral. Approximately 6.5km/4mi; 3h35min. Grade as main walk, but **danger of vertigo.** Access/return, equipment as main walk. Do the main walk, then turn left on the road. The Levada do Curral is 15 minutes downhill. There is a red warning sign here indicating *very dangerous* (see page 36). The path is only 12 inches wide at best, with sheer drops almost immediately. It used to be possible to walk this exceedingly beautiful levada all the way to Funchal (linking up with the second half of Walk 1), but *we no longer recommend it even for experts.* Those with a very good head for heights should be able to follow it for about an hour. Then return the same way to the nearest bus stop.

As recently as the 1950s the post (with vital funds sent home by emigrants) was carried from Funchal to Curral by a woman. Climbing and descending via the Eira, with her precious deliveries balanced in a basket on her head, she counted out 52 hairpin bends each way. We follow the easiest part of her daily round.

Start out at the **Eira do Serrado** (where there is a small hotel under construction). Climb the aloe-fringed path to the famous viewpoint. Then return and descend the steps 3m/10ft to the left of the sign 'EIRA DO SERRADO ALT. 1094 m' (**15min**). The steps lead into a beautiful old cobbled trail below chestnut trees. You clear the trees five minutes down, to be greeted by superb views (*P*3) — and you won't have to

View to Curral das Freiras, near the end of the descent

share them. As the trail makes a U-turn to the left, notice that the road tunnel under the Eira is just opposite you. On the far side of the Ribeira do Curral, the houses of Casas Próximas teeter on the *lombo* plunging off Pico do Serradinho.

As you descend close by the ER107, you'll be a source of some amusement to passing motorists. S-bends take you past a couple of well-placed promontories; one of them (with an electricity pylon; **45min**) is a particularly pleasant picnic spot. From here there is a view back left to the first part of Walk 4: trees mark the Boca da Corrida, and the 'dip' between Pico Grande (with the twin summits) and Pico do Serradinho (to the left) is Boca do Cerro.

Beyond this promontory the path steepens and drops sharply in more S-bends. It is narrow in places, and you may need to use your hands to cross stabilised rock-falls. In summer the surrounding cliffs are bright with yellow-flowering houseleeks. On coming to cultivated terraces (**1h15min**), you're just opposite Curral's church. When the road is just below you, notice that the path *climbs*; don't try to scramble down too soon. Once on the ROAD (**1h20min**), turn left downhill to the nearby BUS STOP or descend to the levada (Alternative walk). Or walk uphill to Curral (15min).

Walk 4: the massive escarpment of Pico Grande, seen ahead, will rise 300m/1000ft sheer above us beyond the Boca do Cerro.

4 BOCA DA CORRIDA • PICO GRANDE • ENCUMEADA

Map on reverse of the touring map; photograph opposite

Distance: 14km/8.7mi; 4h10min

Grade: moderate ups and downs, with an overall climb of about 300m/1000ft and descent of 500m/1650ft; you must be sure-footed. Below the escarpment of Pico Grande the path is narrow (**possibility of vertigo**), often wet, and *sometimes impassable*, due to landslides.

Equipment: walking boots, long trousers, sunhat, picnic, plastic bottle/water purifying tablets, whistle; extra cardigans, anorak in cool weather

How to get there: 🚌 any of the many buses to Estreito de Câmara de Lobos; then taxi to Boca da Corrida
To return: 🚌 6 from Encumeada

Alternative walk: Boca da Corrida — Boca do Cerro — Corticeiras. 11.5km/7mi; 3h30min. Fairly easy. Stout shoes, sunhat, picnic, water. Access as for main walk; return on 🚌 96. Follow the main walk to Boca do Cerro; then return to Boca da Corrida and walk down the road from the forestry house. Just 1km beyond the Quinta do Jardim da Serra (photograph page 24), at a junction with signposting to 'Foro' and 'Jardim da Serra', you can catch a 96 'Foro' bus. Otherwise, turn left uphill for 400m/yds, to the Pastelaria Santiago in Corticeiras, where the 96 'Corticeiras' bus stops. Or 🚗 to/from Boca da Corrida *(limited parking);* this shortens the walk by 4.5km/1h10min.

If we had to choose our favourite mountain walk on the island, it would probably be this one. There is so much to recommend it: not only are the views magnificent throughout, but there's very little climbing! The first part of the walk, to the Boca do Cerro, is still fairly easy, despite the fact that the once-grassy trail has been badly eroded by groups of walkers in recent years. Rounding Pico Grande can sometimes be tricky, but most of the time the path is safe, and few people will find it vertiginous.

At the pass of **Boca da Corrida** there is a forestry house, a shrine, and a spectacular viewpoint over Curral das Freiras. Pico Grande rises ahead of you here. It's John's favourite mountain and easily identified from all over the island because of the rocky knoll on its summit. To the left of it you'll see a path, but this is *not* our path. Our route is higher and, for the moment, hidden from view; it runs just above the layer of broom, at the foot of the rock face with fencing.

Begin the walk by taking the stone-laid trail at the left of the SHRINE. Almost at once turn right (ignore the concreted track on the left between pillars; it is the route followed by Alternative walk 5 from the Casas do Dr Alberto). Then fork left on a stony path marked with an orange stripe and a star (see page 36). You climb a rough trail, eventually passing to the right of the fencing you spotted from the pass. After **8min** the walk levels out and, from a promontory on the right, there are fine views of the high mountains towering above Curral. The Vinháticos *pousada* and the Paúl da Serra come into focus from the **Boca dos Corgos**, a pass reached in **30min**. (Be sure to ignore the old trail down sharp left to Serra de Água here; the last time we looked, it petered out lower down.) Five minutes later you go through a gate, and soon the workmen's house on the Levada do Norte at Encumeada can be seen — as well as the entire Paúl da Serra plateau. In **45min**, another gate marks the **Passo de Ares**.

At **1h10min** reach a gate leading to the fourth pass, the **Boca do Cerro**.* *(The Alternative walk turns back here.)* Beyond the Boca do Cerro, our route (which was the main north/south trail over the island in the 1800s) narrows appreciably, but it is easily discernible. Turn down left through the prickly gorse (sign with an orange stripe and three stars) and soon begin to skirt the awe-inspiring escarpment of **Pico Grande**. It will take a good 20 minutes to pass this rock face, where the *path is very narrow, often wet, and prone to landslides.* Then the generally narrow route begins its descent to Encumeada.

Beyond the **Fenda do Ferreiro**, you reach a wide promontory (**2h**), from where the views towards the Paúl da Serra and down to the Pousada dos Vinháticos are especially fine. In **2h35min**, where there is a U-turn in the path, you may see a sign pointing back to Estreito. Ten minutes later, ignore a path down to the left. At about **2h50min** you will come into the enchanting valley of the **Ribeira do Poço**, emerald green and bright with *poios* and *palheiros*.

Cross a grass-covered stone bridge in **3h**, and ignore any paths downhill to the left. At **3h55min**, you pass under the pipe carrying water from the Norte and Rabaças levadas (Walk 32) down to the power station at Serra de Água. A rough track eventually comes underfoot, and the Residencial Encumeada can be seen below. You soon meet the ER228 (**4h10min**). Wait for the bus here: flag it down! Better still, if you have time, walk 1km downhill to the *residencial* (10min), for a refreshing drink or snack.

---

*From the Boca do Cerro *experts* can scramble to the summit of Pico Grande (1h30min return) or descend to Curral (3h). Note the warning sign here (red stripe with three stars). The Pico Grande path forks left off the Curral path towards some wooden sheep pens, to climb the eastern flanks of the mountain, but it soon fades, and you must make your own way to the top. *Reckon on mists! Set up markers for your descent!* Both this descent and the descent to Curral involve short stretches on narrow ledges — plenty of 'exposure'. Both paths are viable for *expert* mountain walkers with a head for heights, but there is *no* protective fencing. These routes are shown on the map, but not highlighted in colour.

5 FONTES • ACHADA DA PINTA • TROMPICA • FONTES

Map on reverse of touring map

Distance: 11km/6.8mi; 3h35min

Grade: moderate climb and descent of 500m/1650ft on track. The initial ascent is tiring in hot weather.

Equipment: stout shoes (walking boots preferable), sunhat, picnic, water; extra cardigan and anorak in cool weather

How to get there and return: 🚌 to Fontes, above Boa Morte. Turn off the ER229 at the KM172 marker, signposted 'S João, S Paulo'. Beyond Boa Morte, cross the Levada do Norte in the pine forest (3.5km from the ER229), then continue north. Round the deep valley of the Ribeira Funda, ignore the turning left for Espigão, and drive past the impressive steps to São Paulo's church. Fontes is the next hamlet, 1.4km north. Leave your car parked well off the road, so that the bus or any heavy lorry can turn round. Fontes is also accessible by 🚌 127 *from Ribeira Brava*.

Alternative walk: Fontes — Achada da Pinta — Trompica — Boca da Corrida — Corticeiras. 15.5km/9.6mi; 5h40min. *A more attractive return route than the track used in the main walk and especially recommended for those travelling by bus.* Moderate, but you must be surefooted on the path in the Ribeira do Campanário. Equipment as above, but walking boots and long trousers recommended. Access by 🚌 127 or taxi; return on 🚌 96 from Corticeiras. At the Trompica forestry house (2h50min), climb up the earthen bank at the left of the track, to find a good but narrow path which circles the Ribeira do Campanário. If you come to any forks, be prepared to spend a few minutes searching out the correct, well-trodden path (it may be overgrown, depending on the season) and remember not to lose height. Some 20min from Trompica you'll be at the centre of the valley, with a photogenic cultivated knoll below you. Soon there is a delightful grove above the path, on the left. Two river tributaries, with lovely rock pools, are crossed on stepping stones and, in 40min, you reach the lowest of the 'Casas do Dr Alberto' (you will have spotted the three buildings on the property on your approach). Climb straight ahead here, at the left-hand side of this lowest stone shed. You come to the highest building, where you meet a track. Turn right on this track for Boca da Corrida. Another track comes in from above you, on your left, in about 1h10min, and you reach the forestry house at Boca da Corrida 1h40min from Trompica (4h30min). From here walk down the road from the forestry house. Just 1km beyond the Quinta do Jardim da Serra (photograph page 24), at a junction with signposting to 'Foro'

Casa do Dr Alberto
(Alternative walk)

and 'Jardim da Serra', you can catch a 96 'Foro' bus. Otherwise, turn left uphill for 400m/yds, to the Pastelaria Santiago in Corticeiras, where the 96 'Corticeiras' bus stops. *Special note: The path in the Campanário Valley is grazed by cows; we have often encountered up to a dozen on the narrow path. Be prepared to lose time here, shooing them away **quietly**. Approach the Casas do Dr Alberto quietly, too: one of the houses is inhabited, and the lands are farmed by a charming man. Please protect the friendly welcome you will receive here for future walkers.*

H ere's a walk that shows you the great divide formed by the Ribeira Brava from a new perspective. Not only will you have fantastic views over the north/south cleft of this deep ravine, but the panorama encompasses all the great peaks (Walks 19 and 20), Pico Grande (Walk 4), and the entire eastern escarpment of the Paúl da Serra. What's more, this is one of the few island walks that we can whole-heartedly recommend as a varied and satisfying circuit for those with hired cars.

At **Fontes** the asphalt road swings round to the right, but a concrete track rises at the right-hand side of the bar/shop (at the left of the 'Fontes' sign). **Start out** by climbing this track. It's a steep haul, especially tiring in hot weather, and there is *no shade*. But *don't* be discouraged by the dusty climb; once you reach the first pass, the way will become grassy and remain so for most of the walk.

The route takes you up the right-hand side of the **Ribeira Grande**. Within **35min** you will have crossed the **Ribeiro Frio** and be aiming for the first pass. On reaching it, the way becomes grassy. Look back to see the village of São Paulo. Small herds of cows will be encountered throughout the walk, grazing freely on this relatively level terrain.

Within **50min**, at another pass, you begin to enjoy the best views on the walk — the Ribeira Brava basin comes into sight, as well as the Lombo do Mouro (Walk 31), Vinháticos,

From fields of foxgloves and broom you look back down to São Paulo.

Pináculo (Walk 33), and Encumeada. As you round **Pico da Cruz** (**1h**), be sure to keep right (due south) on the track, where a path descends to the left. The grassy track takes you through fields of spring-blooming thistles, foxgloves and broom; a meadow lies below. In the past barley was grown up here (the reason for cutting the track), but it did not flourish. Yet another pass, reached in **1h10min**, opens up more views to the great peaks, from Grande round to Ruivo, via Pico do Gato and the Torres.

Beyond another pass, at about **1h25min**, you come to a Y-fork. The track to the right is the return route but, for the moment, go straight ahead. Some 15 minutes later (**1h40min**) a fence is encountered; here a makeshift stile must be negotiated. Seven minutes later the track makes a 90° turn to the left and ends at a pass (**1h50min**). Climb up half-right towards the summit. You will reach a small rock enclosure on the **Achada da Pinta** within seven minutes. At the far right-hand corner, stones have been placed to allow you to climb over carefully, without disturbing the wall. Inside the enclosure is a triangulation point, where a blue 'hat' is painted on the concrete — a fanatical Madeiran walker's way of saying 'Kilroy was here' (you will see these blue 'hats' on almost all your walks). From here you have a new outlook — over Curral's setting and even down to Funchal.

Leave the triangulation point by climbing over the wall where you came in and retrace your steps to the fork first met in 1h25min (**2h25min**). Turn down sharp left. The track descends through a couple of gates and past minor tracks to the right and the left, which you ignore. By **2h45min** you're walking beneath sweet chestnuts and eucalyptus, but the track is no longer grassy. Five minutes later (**2h50min**) the **Trompica** forestry house is met, on your right. (Here the Alternative walk leaves us, by taking the path up to the left of the track.)

Continue down past the forestry house on the track. Allow 45 minutes for the tedious return to Fontes. Some 30 minutes below Trompica you come to T-junction with an asphalt road.* Keep right here (left goes to Lugar da Serra and Campanário), descending at first, then climbing gently back to **Fontes**, 1km away (**3h35min**).

*A very short section of this road is not shown on our *walking* map; see the touring map or the walking map on pages 54-55.

6 LEVADA DO NORTE: FROM ESTREITO DE CÂMARA DE LOBOS TO BARREIRAS

Distance: 21km/13mi; 6h

Grade: easy, but long; a few sections demand a head for heights

Equipment: stout shoes, sunhat, picnic, water, torch; extra cardigan and anorak in cool weather

How to get there: 🚌 96 to the levada crossing, 0.7km north of Estreito's church; ask for the 'Levada do Norte' bus stop.

To return: 🚌 4, 6, 7, 80, 107, 115, 127 or 148 from Barreiras

Short walks

1 Estreito — first waterhouse. 6.5km/4mi; 1h40min. Easy, but some narrow stretches demand a head for heights. Equipment and access as main walk. Follow the main walk for 1h35min and catch one of the frequent buses on the ER229. This can easily be extended to visit the Cabo Girão viewpoint: continue on the levada to the tunnel (the 1h 55min-point) but, instead of curving right through it, keep ahead alongside a narrow levada. You will pass two steeply-stepped paths down towards Câmara de Lobos. When you come to a road, follow it 500m/yds uphill to the right, to the viewpoint (about 25min from the tunnel). If no 🚌 154 is due, walk back down to the ER229.

2 Quinta Grande — Campanário. 8km/5mi; 2h. Grade and equipment as main walk. Access: 🚌 4, 6, 7, 107, 115, 123, 139, or 142 to 'Ribeira da Quinta Grande', where the ER229 crosses the levada. Follow the main walk from the 2h10min-point to the 3h45min-point, then descend to the ER229 at Campanário (frequent buses).

3 Boa Morte circuit. 3.5km/2.2mi; 1h. Easy; *highly recommended for beginners or people with hired cars.* Wear sensible shoes and take a picnic. Access/return: any 🚌 to Ribeira Brava, then 🚌 127 to Boa Morte. From Boa Morte follow the road uphill to the levada in the pine forest and turn left along it (*P*6), picking up the main walk at the 4h35min-point. You'll be back in Boa Morte in time for 🚌 148. 🚗: If travelling by car, you can park beside the levada. Turn off the ER229 for 'S João, S Paulo'. Drive through Boa Morte and continue to the levada in the pine forest; park on one of the tracks (3.5km uphill from the ER229).

Alternative ending: The 2000 steps. *Sure-footed* walkers can end the main walk or Short walk 3 with a truly *spectacular* descent (walking stick recommended). Continue on the levada past the concrete balcony (4h52min), with more wonderful views over the valley. Ignore a path down left, cross a stream and, 25 minutes along, cross over a path with street lights. Some 12 minutes later, by a waterhouse, you come to concrete steps, just above the village of Eira do Mourão. Well over 2000 steep steps will take you down 500m/1650ft to Fajã on the ER104, where you could catch 🚌 6. Allow 1h30min for this descent (a total time of 7h for the main walk or 2h35min for Short walk 3). But if you have missed the bus, you will have to walk another 2km south into Ribeira Brava.

A ll year round this is a superb walk through a landscape rich in cultivation, thanks to the waters of the Levada do Norte (see notes in Walk 32). Here in early autumn the grapes are harvested for some of Madeira's best-known wines, and the valleys are thick with sugar cane and cherry trees.

When the bus roars up the hill at Estreito, you'll first pass the church and then a chapel on the left. Just round the next bend is the BUS STOP, called 'Levada (do Norte)'. **The walk starts** here, on the west side of the road, where you climb a few steps up to the levada, hidden under concrete at first, and covered by vine-bearing trellises. You'll hear it singing underfoot and reach the end of the covered walkway in **4min**. Look left soon for good views of São Martinho Church and, on a clear day, the Desertas Islands.

At about **20min**, as you enter the narrow **Ribeira da Caixa**, be sure to take a short diversionary path down and round a dangerous part of the levada (marked with a red arrow). Soon you'll find yourself deep in the valley; in spring it is smothered in cherry blossoms. You cross a tributary on a levada bridge in **35min** and then the main river in **45min**.

On leaving the valley, start counting churches to measure your progress. At **1h05min** here's the first, below at **Garachico** (see opposite). A large grey and white waterhouse is met at **1h35min**. Descend steps on the left here and, when you meet a road, climb it to regain the levada. *(But end Short walk 1 by turning left on the road, down to the ER229.)*

Staying on the levada, you must follow a stabilised path over a landslide (1999) caused by the factory up to the right. (Or, to avoid this, walk down to the ER229 and follow it to the right, until you see concrete steps on the left back down to the levada.) In six to seven minutes you cross the ER229. Drawing ever closer to Cabo Girão, enjoy the splendid views of the coast above **Caldeira**. Just before you go through the Cabo Girão tunnel at **Cruz da Caldeira (1h55min)**, some sheer drops are encountered, but they are protected by railings. (You may wish to take a detour here to Cabo Girão; see notes

for Short walk 1 on page 54.) It only takes three minutes to walk through this tunnel and it *can* be managed without a torch, since the path is wide and the roof is high. Now Cabo Girão has disappeared, and you're in the **Ribeira da Quinta Grande**. At **2h10min** the levada skirts the river bridge below the ER229. *Before you reach the parapet,* climb right up a dirt path to the main road. (*Short walk 2 begins here on the west side of the road,*

Boa Morte pine forest

The splendid vineyards below the church at Garachico

where the levada is covered with concrete for a short distance; deduct 2h10min from times below.)

At **2h25min** count the second church — at **Quinta Grande** — as you continue along another high and narrow stretch, parallel with the ER229. Soon come to a spot that's exceptionally lovely in the autumn: stately pillars of pine and sweet chestnut stand proud in iron-rich soil. The forest is alive with pink belladonna lilies. Further on, the houses are festooned with dahlias and the aroma of wood fires is in the air. On roof-tops, marrows and beans almost strangle the charming chimneys.

Count the church of Campanário off to the west and start heading up the valley of the **Ribeira do Campanário**, golden with gorse and broom in spring. At about **3h10min** there are some very severe drops to the left, but they are secured by heavy iron railings. Soon you see the ER229 above Campanário — the square-shaped U-turn is very easily recognised. Cross the Ribeira do Campanário on a levada bridge in an ivy-creepered nook (**3h35min**).

Continue through the wooded heights above **Campanário** and in 10 minutes (**3h45min**) you'll cross a dirt track. (*If you are doing Short walk 2, leave here:* go straight down the track — do not take the left-hand fork. Descend to the ER229, where you'll find a bus stop and a bar/shop.)

Those continuing on the levada will cross a concrete lane beside a first waterhouse and then the tarred road to Lugar da Serra at **4h10min**. A football pitch is just below the levada, on the east side of the road. Eight minutes later pass a lovely little ruin on the right, with a grassy *poio* and chestnut trees — a delightful spot for a break. Soon you enjoy a fine view over the graceful arc of the expressway.

A large waterhouse is met in the Boa Morte pine forest; just beyond it is the road down to the village (**4h35min**; *Short walk 3 comes in here*). Cross the road (a bar/café is down to the left) and continue in the exceptionally beautiful setting shown opposite (*P*6): the levada mirrors the trees, and the path is soft with pine needles.

Some 12-13 minutes after crossing the Boa Morte road, note a dirt track off left (**4h48min**). For the moment pass it by; in **4h52min** you come to a concrete balcony, looking out over the great cleft of the Ribeira Brava, its terraces, poplars, and banana plantations. The views north and south are magnificent (**P**6). This levada flows from far, far north of the viewpoint. (You could easily follow it to Eira do Mourão for the 'Alternative ending', or go as far as the first tunnel (1h), but the path will become extremely vertiginous, and there is no protective fencing. *Experts:* it's 13km/8mi; 4h30min of almost constant 'exposure' — or long tunnels! — from here to the power station at Serra de Água; a torch is essential.)

Return from the concrete balcony to the track first passed at 4h48min and descend to **Boa Morte** (**5h20min**). It's unlikely you will be in time to catch the last bus of the day, so walk down to the ER229 at **Barreiras** (**6h**). The BUS SHELTER is opposite.

Eira do Mourão (Alternative descent) and the Ribeira Brava Valley

7 LEVADA DOS TORNOS: FROM ROMEIROS TO THE SÍTIO DAS QUATRO ESTRADAS

Distance: 27.5km/17mi; 7h30min (but see Short walks below).

Grade, equipment, how to get there and return: see Short walks.

Short walks: This walk breaks conveniently into the four stages described below. We begin at Romeiros, to avoid climbing to the levada. If you wish to begin at Monte or Babosas (a small square and viewpoint with a bus terminus), follow the purple line on the map. The path to Romeiros leaves Babosas between the chapel shown on page 65 and the concrete seats at the viewpoint. *Important note:* 350m/yds below Babosas, **there is a critical choice of paths.** *All walkers except experts should* **keep right downhill on the cobbled trail with street lights;** it will take you to Romeiros, where you can pick up Short walk 1 (page 60). *Experts with no fear of heights* may like to keep left uphill on the earthen path here. This path will climb to join the levada at the point where it emerges from a tunnel *(very long stretches of sheer unprotected drops).*

1 Romeiros — Palheiro Ferreiro. 6km/3.7mi; 1h30min. Easy. Stout shoes, sunhat, picnic, water. *Town* 🚌 29 to Romeiros; return from the the levada crossing on the ER102 at Palheiro Ferreiro on 🚌 29 or 77 or *town* 🚌 37. (Or stop at one of the two tea houses en route and return on *town* 🚌 47.) Notes begin on page 60. If you want to visit the Palheiro Gardens first (open 09.30-12.30 Mon-Fri, except holidays; *town* 🚌 36), do the walk in reverse. Walk back to the main Gardens entrance, then turn right and climb the ER102 for about 10 minutes, to where it crosses the levada (just behind the school). Turn left on the levada and follow it to Romeiros, a village where the levada is covered by concrete paving. Here steps take you down left off the levada, to avoid a building with a flagpole. You drop 4m/12ft, to a cobbled trail. Turn left and follow the trail down to the terminus of *town* 🚌 29. Or, to continue to Monte, turn *right* on the cobbled trail, walking *below* the building with a flagpole. Follow the street lights all the way to Babosas and then Monte.

2 Palheiro Ferreiro — Camacha. 5.5km/3.4mi; 1h40min. Easy, but there is a very awkward tunnel (10 minutes). Stout shoes (boots preferable), sunhat, picnic, water and a *good torch* for each member of the party. *Town* 🚌 37 or 🚌 29 or 77 to the ER102 at Palheiro Ferreiro; ask for 'Levada dos Tornos'. Return from Camacha on 🚌 29 or 77 (or from Nogueira on 🚌 110 or 114). Notes begin on page 63.

3 Camacha — Lombo Grande. 6km/3.7mi; 1h30min. Easy, but *you must be sure-footed, and there is a* **danger of vertigo***:* the path is very narrow in places. Blackberry thorns sometimes intrude, and you may have to walk *through* (seasonal) waterfalls. Equipment as for Short walk 2 above, plus extra cardigan, long trousers, anorak in cool weather, whistle. *Don't forget the torches!* 🚌 29 or 77 to Camacha; return from Lombo Grande on 🚌 60, or walk 1km uphill to Boqueirão for 🚌 110 or 1.6km uphill to Águas Mansas for 🚌 77. Notes begin on page 64.

4 Lombo Grande — Sítio das Quatro Estradas. 11.5km/7.1mi; 3h. Grade and equipment as Short walk 3, **but this stretch of levada is even more vertiginous** and there is a tiring climb of 150m/500ft to the Sítio das Quatro Estradas. Access: 🚌 60 (ask for 'Levada dos Tornos, Lombo Grande'). From the bus stop, walk north up the ER206 for one minute to the levada. Or 🚌 77 to Águas Mansas or 🚌 110 to Boqueirão, then walk down to the levada (1.6km below Águas Mansas). Notes page 65.

Alternative walks: You could join Walk 8, 9 or 10. You shouldn't have any difficulty, either, reversing Short walks 1, 2 or 3 (route-finding on Short walk 4, however, would be very difficult in reverse).

The pull-out touring map gives you a good overview of the **Levada dos Tornos**. Inaugurated in 1966, it is Madeira's most important levada, with 106km (66mi) of main channels. Water collected from three chief sources in the north flows to the power station at Fajã da Nogueira. (You can explore the northern reaches of the Tornos on Walks 23 and 24.)

From the power station at Fajã da Nogueira (Walk 24) the levada flows through a very long tunnel (there are 16km/10mi of tunnels on the Tornos!) to the south of the island. It emerges into the open in the upper reaches of the João Gomes Valley, north of Romeiros, and then meanders on to irrigate more than 100,000 outlets between Funchal and Santa Cruz. And it is this southern run of the Tornos that we describe in the walk*. From a height of 600 metres (almost 2000 feet) the hustle and bustle of life at sea level seems very far away; walking this levada path is like overflying the south coast in a balloon.

Start Short walk 1 at the BUS TERMINUS in **Romeiros**. Climb steps and then the concrete path on the west side of the turning circle for the bus. Just where the concrete ends and cobbles begin, turn right, up concrete steps. (*If you pass below a building with a flagpole, you have gone too far.*) At the top of the steps, you are on the levada, but it is covered with concrete. Turn right on this covered walkway; you'll soon see the levada in full flow.

*We begin 1.3km southeast of where the levada leaves the tunnel in the João Gomes Valley — not only to avoid a stiff climb, but because the path near the tunnel is so vertiginous. *Experts, with no fear of unprotected precipices, could begin at Monte or Babosas (see page 59).*

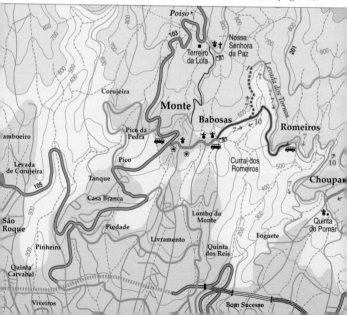

Follow the levada through groves of pine and mimosa and, in **35min**, you'll cross a narrow tarred road. Go through the gate opposite. A delightful chapel is on your right. This is the QUINTA DO POMAR. The building itself is fenced off; to avoid the narrow levada channel behind it, go left on the footpath which quickly takes you back to the levada. In about **1h** you pass steps up left to a stop for town bus 47. Some 200m/yds further on, more steps lead up left to the HORTENSIA tea house, in beautifully-landscaped gardens. Cross the ER201 (**1h10min**) and, three minutes later, pass above the JASMIN tea house. In **1h30min** you reach the ER102. Approach *carefully* — traffic roars round the blind bend to the left. *(Short walk 1 ends here; follow this busy road 200m/yds downhill to the right, to a bus shelter.* The PALHEIRO GARDENS are several minutes further downhill, on the left, almost opposite the ER201 to Terreiro da Luta — and another BUS STOP).

Short walk 2 begins at the **Levada dos Tornos** BUS STOP (no *paragem* sign). The levada is just by the stop. Head east in a delightful setting, bright with flowers and ochre-red soil. Almost at once you overlook **Palheiro Ferreiro**, the south coast, and the Desertas Islands. In three minutes you pass a school on your right. Walk to the left of another large building; a small stadium is above you, on the left. Cross a road and rejoin the levada by turning *sharp* left. Fragrant mimosa and eucalyptus grace the next stretch.

In **20min** you come to a tunnel. *Watch your head: the vaulting is low and jagged.* (The path to the right of the tunnel would take you uphill to a bar/shop, but you would have a very slippery descent back to the levada. This route is highlighted in purple on the map, but we recommend going through the tunnel.) You emerge 10 minutes later, soon coming to pleasant pine groves.

As you enter the **Ribeira do Caniço**, sprinkled with apple blossom in spring, look to the far side: you will see a road with street lights. When you come into the village of **Nogueira**, you must leave the levada: go left up concrete steps to join this road and follow it to the right uphill. There are fine views down right over Caniço. As you come into a large housing estate, ignore all crossroads and keep ahead uphill. Pass a stop sign and walk ahead past the TERMINUS FOR BUS 114 to a T-junction with the ER205 (Caniço road; **1h05min**). Turn left here past the Laboratório Agricola but, one minute uphill, just at the boundary of the laboratory, turn right on a road. Go straight over a crossroads, down into the village of **Ribeirinha** (where there is a stop for the No 111 bus). Then follow the road across a bridge and up out of Ribeirinha's valley*, to a T-junction. Go left uphill here, with glimpses down right over the Porto Novo Valley. Ignore a tarred road off to the right; keep left and, at the next T-junction, go right. You come into **Camacha** by the village square, the Achada da Camacha (**1h40min**), where the CAFÉ/ESTALAGEM DO RELÓGIO is on your right.

Start Short walk 3 facing the CAFÉ/ESTALAGEM DO RELÓGIO in **Camacha**'s square (Achada da Camacha). Descend the road at the right of the café (a bank is on your right). Ignore a small road off right and, at the next fork, go left downhill. In **7min** fork right and then look left for a fine view over the Porto Novo. A few minutes later, turn left at a T-junction. In under **15min** you meet the **Levada dos Tornos**: turn left.

Having passed a house with a large palm tree (**23min**)**, you come to a tunnel a minute later. You'll need your torch, although it takes only three minutes to get through. Another tunnel is met in **40min** (two minutes; no torch needed). Beyond this tunnel there is a possibility of vertigo for, although the levada path is very adequate, there is no protective fencing, and the drops are severe — perhaps 50m/ 150ft. Often waterfalls cascade onto the path as well, and you may get soaked. Watch out, too, for the concrete blocks in the path, supporting the pipe carrying some of the water. Still, we hope you will manage this part of the walk in the lower part of the **Ribeira do Porto Novo** (see also Walk 8), because it is one of the most beautiful stretches of the Tornos. Suddenly birds and cascades are singing everywhere. In **50min** the levada makes a U-turn high in the valley, below some pools. The waterfall shown opposite crashes into the river; all else is stillness. This is an idyllic picnic spot.

Eight minutes from the pools you pass a dyke on the right and a *palheiro*. Pass through the third and shortest tunnel (**1h**), before skirting round a tunnel with 'windows' at about **1h10min** (be sure to climb up steps beyond this tunnel to rejoin the Tornos; the levada continuing ahead runs down to Gaula). This is another lovely picnic spot (*P*7a). Across the valley you can see Salgados, dribbling down the ridge (Walk 8). All too soon, you reach a reservoir at **Lombo Grande**.

*Or, to continue on the levada, watch for a large white arrow signpost 'Levada dos Tornos' (it *may* be hidden in greenery) on your right, as the road climbs out of Ribeirinha (50-100m/yds past the bridge). Take this path. At a first fork, ignore a path off to the right; keep straight ahead. Over to the right is a beautiful old rose-painted house with a timbered balcony. Five minutes off the road, at a Y-fork, bear right. You reach the levada in a minute: turn left (or first turn right, if you want to take a closer look at the balconied house). When you come to a house with a large palm tree, pick up the notes for Short walk 3 above, at the 23min-point.

**The cobbled road at the palm tree house first descends a bit, then rises to a T-junction, where a right turn leads to the 10min-point in Walk 8.

Along the Tornos (clockwise): old house at Nogueira, waterfall at the head of the Porto Novo Valley, flower-filled channel near Romeiros, pink house at Ribeirinha (see first footnote opposite), statue at the Quinta do Pomar, and chapel at Babosas (alternative starting point).

Beyond it is the ER206 (just over **1h30min**). Turn right and descend for under a minute to the BUS STOP.

   Short walk 4 begins where the ER206 crosses the levada at **Lombo Grande**. Head east; in under **10min** you have good views over the airport and São Lourenço Point. After **20min** you pass through a very short tunnel (no torch is needed, but it is very low: watch your head!) and come out in the **Ribeira da Boaventura** (*P*7b). While the Porto Novo is our favourite part of the Tornos in spring, in summer the Boaventura Valley (see page 66) takes the prize. The terraces are golden with wheat, and the levada paths are aglow with blue and white agapanthus — so tall and thick that they are almost like hedgerows. Most walkers will have no difficulty following the levada for a good 20 minutes past the tunnel, but then the way becomes vertiginous, as it delves into a very deep tributary, the **Ribeira dos Vinháticos**. By **50min** you reach the head of this stream. The next, smaller tributary, is a basin full of willow. In just over **1h35min** you pass a waterhouse on the left; beyond it is an asphalt road. Two minutes later a second asphalt road is crossed (**1h40min**). Both lead up to the ER102 at João Frino, if you're pressed for time and trying to catch bus 77. Beyond the second road you delve into the upper reaches of a new valley — the **Ribeira de Santa Cruz**. Ignore all the cobbled trails and paths crossing the levada during the next 45 minutes or so; civilisation seems very far away, as you enter an emerald wilderness.

   Then suddenly, at **2h25min**, the levada ends. Unbelievable! How can this magnificent watercourse, which has

Picnic 7b, in the upper Boaventura Valley, looks out to these colourful terraces, spilling down a ridge between the Vinháticos and João Frino rivers.

carried you through the most beautiful valleys in the southeast, have abandoned you without warning? Its waters shoot out into a tank some 200m/650ft below, to feed the Levada Nova (see Walk 9). A pipe coming in from the Levada da Serra (Walk 10) runs down and over to the *lagoa* (reservoir) above Santo da Serra.

Walk back along the levada. In two minutes you pass a narrow path on the left (Walk 9 ascends it, from the Levada Nova; the descent is *not* recommended). Four minutes later, turn right up cobbled steps. A few minutes uphill, you emerge in fields. Head towards the electricity wires in front of you, keeping to the left of the plots. At a stone wall, bear left. Bear left again at a second wall, quickly coming to a cobbled track. Go left uphill (past the entrance to a *quinta*), to a crossroads. Here go straight ahead.* When a tarred road joins you from the left, continue straight ahead (right), climbing to the ER102 at the **Sítio das Quatro Estradas (3h)**. Your BUS SHELTER is across the road.

*If you turn right here, you can follow a track to the church at Santo da Serra (see purple route on the map). You skirt the grounds of the mysterious *quinta*, overgrown with luxuriant vegetation. For a short time in the 1800s it was home to a young Scottish doctor, Robert Reid Kalley, esteemed by the islanders for his near-miraculous cures. But he was also a Protestant, and when the authorities would no longer tolerate his incessant proselytising, he had to flee the island dressed as a woman.

8 CAMACHA • LEVADA DO CANIÇO • ASSOMADA

Map pages 62-63; photo page 16   **Distance:** 6km/3.7mi; 2h20min

Grade: moderate, but with a very steep — sometimes slippery — descent of 250m/820ft to the levada. Surefootedness is essential; **possibility of vertigo** on the levada

Equipment: walking boots, long trousers, sunhat, picnic, water; extra cardigan and anorak in cool weather

How to get there: 🚌 29 or 77 to Camacha
To return: 🚌 2 (or one of many others) from Assomada

Short walk: Assomada — Porto Novo Valley — Assomada. See notes for Picnic 9, page 13.

Alternative walk: Levada dos Tornos — Ribeirinha — Assomada. 11km/ 6.8mi; 3h40min. Grade and equipment as main walk; access as *Short walk 7-2, page 59.* Follow Short walk 7-2 (page 63), but do not climb into Camacha; keep on the levada at Ribeirinha (refer to the first footnote on page 64). When you come to the house with the palm tree, refer to the second footnote on page 64 to join this walk at the 10min-point.

A ny season, any time of day, is suitable for this splendid walk in one of Madeira's most lush valleys. And this is a less vertiginous way to see the lower Porto Novo Valley than by following Walk 7; although the drops on this walk are quite severe, they are not as *sheer,* since there is generally scrub at the edge of the levada path.

Start out facing the CAFÉ/ESTALAGEM DO RELÓGIO in the **Camacha's** square (Achada da Camacha). Walk left round the square, past the viewpoint over the Porto Novo Valley and a chapel. You come to the medical centre (Centro de Saúde): descend the steep tarred lane on the left-hand side of this building. In **10min**, at the school, you meet a fork. *(The Alternative walk joins here.)* Go left on the lily-bordered cobbled path. It descends very steeply into the delightful 'perched' hamlet of **Salgados**, hidden in apple trees and decorated from top to toe with willow.

Following electricity wires, keep on the same path. Pass a TAP on the right, then slither down stone 'steps', which drop you abruptly onto the **Levada do Caniço (35min).** Turn right to ramble to Assomada.

Just beyond a short tunnel, a particularly lovely promontory is met in **1h40min (P8;** see photograph page 16). Here you can picnic nestled in sugar cane, poppies and thistles — while you look out over the valley, the south coast and the Desertas Islands.

In well under **2h**, a concrete path crosses, just before a house. Turn down left; a water channel raised up on pillars is on your left. You reach a road in half a minute. Turn left and follow the road downhill, past an electricity substation on your right. Walk behind the church at **Assomada (2h 20min)** and, on meeting the ER204, turn left. The BUS STOP is in the lay-by on the east side of the church.

9 SANTO DA SERRA • LEVADA NOVA • SÍTIO DAS QUATRO ESTRADAS

Map pages 62-63   **Distance:** 14km/8.7mi; 4h05min

Grade: easy-moderate, with a steep climb of 250m/820ft at the end of the walk. Following the levada, you need to be sure-footed and have a head for heights (**possibility of vertigo**). *Note:* We recommend that you do the walk in the direction described. Trying to descend to the levada from the Sítio das Quatro Estradas is difficult — the path is hard to find and, once you are on it, the descent is very steep and slippery.

Equipment: stout shoes (walking boots preferable), long trousers, sunhat, picnic, water; extra cardigan and anorak in cool weather

How to get there: 🚌 20, 25, 77 or 78 to Santo da Serra (or 🚗). If you object to a long walk on tarmac, take a taxi from there to the Capela dos Cardais, where the levada walk starts (deduct 40min).
To return: 🚌 77 from the Sítio das Quatro Estradas (or same bus or 🚗 from Santo da Serra; add 15min)

Short walk: Santo da Serra — Levada Nova — Sítio das Quatro Estradas (or Santo da Serra). 7km/4.3mi; 2h30min. Grade, equipment, access/return as main walk. Follow the main walk for 6min, but at the Quinta da Paz fork right instead of left. Follow the tarred lane (later concreted) down to the levada, picking up the main walk at the 2h20min-point. This option takes in the loveliest part of the walk.

I f you've walked the Levada dos Tornos from start to finish, wouldn't you think that you'd seen the best of the Santa Cruz Valley? After all, the Tornos is 100m/330ft higher than the Levada Nova. Wouldn't you expect it to be greener, more vertiginous, more beautiful and more exciting than this lower levada? You are in for a surprise!

Start out at the CHURCH in **Santo da Serra**. Follow the ER212 southeast, past the park and a hotel on your left. At the Y-fork in front of the QUINTA DA PAZ (**6min**) bear left. *(But go right for the Short walk).* You pass the golf course on your left and the *lagoa* (reservoir) on the conical hill above right. Beyond the clubhouse for the golf course, you reach another fork. Go left and continue for about eight minutes, to another fork, where you go right. Ten minutes' descent brings you the CAPELA DOS CARDAIS, on your right (**40min**).

The **Levada Nova** lies just above and behind the chapel; join it and head west. The way is graced by *Senecio* and passion flowers, but some blackberry thorns tear at your long trousers too. You cross the ER207 running south to the airport at **1h18min**. Three minutes later, beyond a track, you come to a sizeable piggery. A couple of stone-laid trails cross your way not far beyond here.

Having rounded the **Ribeira do Moreno**, in **2h20min** you meet a concrete road with electricity poles *(the Short walk rejoins here)*. Cross the road; a waterhouse is on your right. The levada is appreciably wider now, as you head up into the **Ribeira de Santa Cruz**. This stretch is guaranteed to delight even the most jaded levada-walker. Masses upon

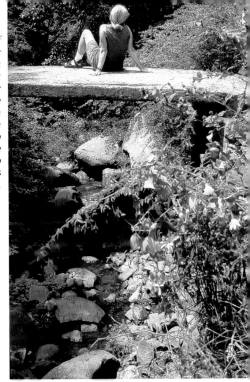

Hidden in a glen of fuchsias, this sliver of a bridge crosses some pretty rock pools in the upper reaches of the Ribeira de Santa Cruz — it's a delightful spot to take a break, before heading back to Santo da Serra's highlands.

masses of blue and white agapanthus dance along the curves of the channel, a waterfall bursts upon the scene and then, in **3h**, you come to an emerald-green fern-covered grotto. But there is more to come: river pools shimmer down to the left, and soon you're in a glen of wild fuchsias. It's all too wonderful to last, and it doesn't. Almost at once the source of the levada is met at a water catchment, where overspill water pours in from the Levada dos Tornos above. A pipe (some of it underground) carries water here from the Levada da Serra (Walk 10) as well. Another pipe, this one visible, runs up to the *lagoa* above Santo da Serra.

From the water catchment, return to a path on your right, just over a minute along, and descend to the bridge shown above. Climb the path on the far side and, at a fork met after only 3-4m/yds, go left. You struggle up to the **Levada dos Tornos** in 15 minutes. Turn right and follow it for two minutes, to where it ends and spills over into the water tank you've just left (**3h30min**). Turn back here and use the notes in the last paragraph on page 66, to climb to the **Sítio das Quatro Estradas** (**4h05min**), or see the footnote on the same page to go direct to Santo da Serra, if you've left your car there (add 1km; 4h20min).

10 LEVADA DA SERRA: FROM CHOUPANA TO PORTELA

Map begins on pages 60-61, continues on pages 62-63, and ends on page 81; photograph page 21

Distance: See introduction and 'The entire length' below.

Grade: easy throughout, but there is always an initial climb to the levada from the bus stop (except for Short walk 1 in reverse). (The ER202 and ER203 also cross the levada, if friends are willing to play taxi; see map.)

Equipment: stout shoes, sunhat, picnic, water; extra cardigans and anorak in cool weather (especially for the stretch north of Camacha)

How to get there and return: See Short walks 1-5 below.

Short walks: See 1-5 below (all are easy).

T he Levada da Serra was our first experience of walking on Madeira, and it may well be yours — especially if you book an 'organised' levada walk. Since much of the way is now signposted, and there is little chance of getting lost, we don't describe the walk in detail. Instead, we tell you how to join the walk at convenient points and do the suggested segments in both directions.

Don't expect to find much water in this levada — most of it has been diverted to the Tornos, some 200m/650ft below (Walk 7). Nor are there many far-reaching views; trees line much of the route. Enjoy instead the flora (hydrangeas, gorse, lilies, rhododendrons — depending on the season) and the pleasant shade of eucalyptus and oak trees. *Do* expect to meet coachloads of walkers ...

The **Levada da Serra** is some 27km/17mi long, from the **Lamaceiros** waterhouse above Portela to its end at **Choupana**, northeast of Romeiros. It can be done in one fell swoop, but it breaks conveniently into five short walks.

The entire length: Choupana — Lamaceiros — Portela. 30km/18.6mi; 8h. Grade: moderate (on account of the length). Take *town* 🚌 47 to the Centro Hípico ('**Sehn**-troh **Hee**-pee-koh'). Continue north along the ER201 for 15 minutes, then climb a steep cobbled trail on your right (opposite the Caminho do Meio). In under eight minutes, a short cobbled path on the right leads to the (dry) levada, which may be hidden by tall grass. Follow the levada all the way to the Lamaceiros waterhouse, then pick up Walk 25 to descend to Portela (🚌 20, 53 or 78). Alternatively, leave at the Santo da Serra waterhouse: descend the track on the south side of this waterhouse to the ER102, where you turn right and then left into Santo da Serra for 🚌 20, 25, 77 or 78 (a somewhat shorter walk of 27km/16.7mi; under 8h). If you do the walk from Portela (see Short walk 5 below), see notes for Short walk 1 to descend from Choupana. *Note:* The levada is covered by a road in the Porto Novo Valley; the short walks omit this stretch.

Short walks

1   Choupana — Achadinha. 7km/4.3mi; 2h10min. Access as 'The entire length'. After crossing the ER203 to Poiso, continue for another 3.5km to Achadinha, where 🚌 111 stops beside the levada. To walk this leg in reverse, take 🚌 111 to the Levada da Serra bus stop at Achadinha. Follow the levada west, crossing the ER203 to Poiso. When the levada ends (at Choupana), turn left down the steep cobbled trail to the ER201 (6min). To catch *town* 🚌 47, turn left: in under 15 minutes you'll come to a stop (near the Hortensia tea house). Or carry on to Monte (add 2h): go straight over the ER201 and descend 500m/yds, to the crossing of the Levada dos Tornos. Turn right on this levada and follow it for 40 minutes to Romeiros, a village where the levada is covered by concrete. Here steps take you down left off the levada, to avoid a building with a flagpole. You drop 4m/12ft, to a cobbled trail. Turn right on the trail, walking *below* the building with a flagpole. Follow the street lights all the way to Babosas (viewpoint and chapel) and then Monte.

2 **Paradise Valley — Camacha.** 6km/3.7mi; 1h40min. Take 🚌 29 or 77 to 'Vale Paraíso' (pronounced '**Val** Pah-rah-**ee**-soh'). Climb the ER203 for 20 minutes to the levada crossing. Turn right. Ignore any forks running down to the right until you come to a crossroads at a group of buildings (some 1h10min along the levada), with signposts on the left for Choupana and Santo da Serra. Turn right downhill. Camacha (🚌 29, 77) is signposted on the building on your right. To do this stretch in reverse, climb the cobbled road north of Camacha's church (where the ER102 forks right to Santo da Serra). Fork left 200m/yds beyond the gates of the Quinta das Almas. At the levada crossing (under 15min), where a signpost indicates 'Choupana', go left. At the crossing of the ER203 to Poiso, turn down left to the ER102, where you can pick up 🚌 29 or 77. Or carry on to Choupana; for transport from there, see Short walk 1.

3 **Águas Mansas — Sítio das Quatro Estradas.** 6km/3.7mi; 1h40min. Take 🚌 77 to Águas Mansas, or 🚌 60 or 110 to Boqueirão (from where you must walk 0.6km uphill to the ER102; add 10min). From the joining of the ER206 and the ER102, walk 100m/yds north towards Santo da Serra, then turn left up a track. You reach the levada in about 10 minutes. Turn right and follow it as far as the ER202 to Poiso; there turn down right to the ER102 to catch 🚌 77 at the Sítio das Quatro Estradas ('place where four roads join'). To do this stretch in reverse, join the levada as in Short walk 4 and turn left. Your descending track to Águas Mansas comes up just before the crossing of the noisy Levada do Pico. *Note:* We do not recommend starting this Short walk at Camacha, because the levada is covered by a road in the Porto Novo Valley.

4 **Sítio das Quatro Estradas — Santo da Serra.** 8km/5mi; 2h20min. Take 🚌 77 to the Sítio das Quatro Estradas ('**See**-tee-oh dahs **Kwa**-troh Esh-**trah**-dahsh'). Climb the ER202 towards Poiso. Just beyond a huge piggery (15min), turn right on the levada (*P*10). About 1h15min later, you cross a track and come to the Santo da Serra waterhouse. Enjoy this charming gardens, then return to the track and descend to the ER102 (25min). Turn right downhill, then turn left into Santo da Serra (20min), to catch 🚌 20, 77 or 78. To do this stretch in reverse, join the levada as in Short walk 5 and turn left. On reaching the crossing of the ER202 to Poiso, turn down left to the ER102, where you can catch 🚌 77.

5 **Santo da Serra — Portela.** 8km/5mi; 2h35min. Take 🚌 20, 77 or 78 to Santo da Serra. From the church walk 500m west to the ER102 and turn right uphill for 300m/yds. Then turn left on a road (later a track) and climb 100m/330ft to the Santo da Serra waterhouse. Turn right and walk to the next waterhouse (Lamaceiros). Now follow Walk 25 (map page 105; notes page106), to Portela. To begin at Portela, walk up the ER102 (signposted to Santo da Serra). Ignore a path right to a shrine but, 150m/yds uphill, climb steps on the right up to the levada (200m/650ft). Follow it to the Lamaceiros waterhouse, but leave it at the next waterhouse (Santo da Serra) descending as in Short walk 4 above.

11 LEVADA DO CANIÇAL: FROM MAROÇOS TO THE CANIÇAL TUNNEL

Map pages 80-81   **Distance:** 11.5km/7.1mi; 3h10min

Grade: easy, after the initial climb of 100 steps to the levada

Equipment: stout shoes, sunhat, long-sleeved shirt, picnic, water; extra cardigan and anorak in cool weather

How to get there: 🚌 156 to Maroços ('Moinhos da Serra' bus)

To return: 🚌 113 from the Pico do Facho bus stop

Short walk: Caniçal tunnel — Boca do Risco — Ribeira Seca. 8.5km/ 5.3mi; 2h10min. Grade and equipment as above. 🚌 113 to the Pico do Facho bus stop on the western side of the Caniçal tunnel. Join the Levada do Caniçal by the waterhouse on the north side of the road and head west. After 35-40min, you meet the path to Boca do Risco: here a path crosses the levada; it leads up from the last house in the valley (with electricity wires). Follow the path up to the right; it's a 30min climb from here to Boca do Risco (see notes pages 79-80; Walk 14). Return the same way and then descend past the house, following the electricity poles down to the road in the valley. Follow it south to the ER109 at Ribeira Seca, where you can catch 🚌 113.

Alternative walk: Maroços to Caniçal. 16km/10mi; 5h05min. Access as above; grade, equipment, return *as Walk 12.* Do the main walk, then continue to Caniçal by following the first half of Walk 12.

The 'mimosa levada' offers an entrancing and easy walk, accessible to most visitors. If you like, you can extend the walk by including a (1h return) detour to Boca do Risco, or you can tack on Walk 12 — going all the way to Caniçal, or just to Pico do Facho and back.

The walk begins at **Maroços** (currently the end of the 156 bus route and 4.3km off the road to Caniçal). With the VILLAGE POST BOXES behind you, walk up the lane between a furniture shop on the left and a garage on the right. This quickly runs into 100 concrete steps which you climb up to the **Levada do Caniçal**. Turn right, to follow the flow of the levada through some enchanting valleys. Notice the fine basalt prisms on the far side of the valley as you start out. You'll

No habitation disturbs the peace in the upper valleys

There is just one tiny cluster of flower-bound houses in the Ribeira Grande, where terracotta birds keep silent watch over the valley.

quickly gain the narrow **Ribeira das Cales**, as you continue through the strung-out village of Maroços. Take heart! Habitation soon ends and, once past Maroços, you come into the **Ribeira Grande** (see right; **50min**) — a first taste of the landscapes that make this walk such a delight.

From now on you will encounter few dwellings until the end of the walk, but the handiwork of the Madeiran farmer is all around. *Palheiros* dot the landscape, mere specks of red and white in the great bowls of greenery. Perhaps you will meet a youngster bringing home a melon — he puts it into the levada and 'steers' it with a stick ... But it is more likely that your only companions will be full-throated frogs singing to their hearts' content.

A short tunnel is met at the end of this valley (**1h05min**; no torch needed) and two minutes later two waterhouses perched up beside the levada. Now we delve into the remote valley shown opposite, the **Ribeira da Noia**. Utterly peaceful, it is perhaps the most beautiful of them all. It soon becomes obvious why we call this the 'mimosa levada'! All year round these golden trees will frame your photographs.

The great cornucopia of the **Ribeira Seca** is reached all too soon. Linger a while beneath some trees; there's a feast for the eyes all around you. From here you can see bright Machico and the Desertas Islands glimmering in the sun. Eight minutes beyond a narrow U-turn in the upper Seca Valley (**2h30min**), you will notice a path crossing the levada. It comes up from the most northerly house in the valley, where there is an electricity pole. This path leads north to Boca do Risco (1h return; notes pages 79-80; Short walk and Walk 14).

Soon you come upon some gorgeous grassy terraces (**P**11), before the way heads back into shade. A waterhouse with brick trellises beside the ER109 marks the end of the walk (**3h10min**). The Caniçal road tunnel is to the left; the bar/restaurant O Tonel is 500m/yds downhill to the right. You can catch a bus here (the Pico do Facho BUS STOP) or walk on to Machico (40min). Better still, if you're properly shod and have a head for heights, cross the main road and climb the Pico do Facho road opposite, to tackle Walk 12!

73

12 PICO DO FACHO — CANIÇAL CIRCUIT

Map pages 76-77   **Distance:** 9km/5.6mi; 3h15min

Grade: moderate, with overall ascents/descents of about 300m/1000ft; you must be sure-footed and have a head for heights (**danger of vertigo**).

Equipment: walking boots, sunhat, long-sleeved shirt, long trousers, picnic, water

How to get there and return: 🚌 113 to/from the Caniçal tunnel: alight at the western end and return the eastern end. 🚗 By car, park well tucked in at the side of the road to Pico do Facho (or start at Caniçal).

Short walks: Do either half of the main walk, ending at or starting from the church in Caniçal. Grade and equipment as above. About 1h30min.

This invigorating hike first takes you high above the sea, with fine views to São Lourenço. You'll cross grassy terraces veined with old stone walls and then follow an narrow, often precipitous path — once it was a wide mule trail serving the now mostly-abandoned terraces. The second half of the walk follows a narrow levada through some delightful woodlands, before making a dramatic descent to the main road.

Start out at the **Pico do Facho** BUS STOP on the west side of the CANIÇAL TUNNEL. Climb the road towards the peak. Electricity pylons will guide you from here to Caniçal: *take note of them!* The first pylon comes up just before the peak (**20min**): leave the road here and walk left through a rubbish tip. Beyond the tip, at a Y-fork of paths, bear right. Now you'll see a second pylon ahead. Your path passes well above it, at the top of some still-cultivated terraces. It takes you straight to the third pylon (**35min**). Here, on a ridge between the **Ilhéu** and **Pejal** streams, you enjoy first views of Caniçal.

Now the path unexpectedly turns *inland.* Go left up bedrock and after 20 paces fork right. Ten minutes later (**45min**) the fourth pylon is about 150m/yds ahead of you. ***Watch out here.*** Do *not* follow the path towards this pylon. The path you want (not easily seen at first) turns off to the right and runs about 20m/60ft *below* the pylon and rounds it on the sea side, zigzagging and dropping considerably. When you come to the next bedrock area at a precipice (**50min**), the path bends sharply to the left. You overlook Caniçal here. Ten minutes from this precipice, you pass to the left of the fifth pylon (**1h05min**), from where the end of the walk is in view. Looking inland, you spot a beautiful old humpback footbridge over the **Natal** stream below. The path takes you down to it — a scramble involving all fours. Once over the BRIDGE (**1h15min**), turn left uphill on a track. As a fence looms, turn right downhill in front of it. Keep this fence beside you on your left almost all the way to the westernmost quay at **Caniçal**; here tar comes underfoot. Continue straight ahead along the front, heading for the Shell petrol station. Turn left uphill in front of it, pass the whaling museum, and continue to the CHURCH/BUS STOP (**1h30min**).

Head east from the church on the main street, then take the second left turn (opposite the Bar Estrela do Mar). Cross straight over the main road which leads to Baía da Abra; the 'Correos' building will be on your right (**1h45min**). Climb the road opposite; a green wire fence is on the right. The road soon reverts to track, and the fencing ends, as the track makes for the wood ahead. To mitigate the tedious climb, enjoy the view over right to some wonderful volcanic rock in hues of reds, yellows, golds and greens. Keep beside the gutter at the left of the road; it leads you to the narrow **Levada do Caniçal**, which soon enters the wood (**2h05min**) and continues uphill through mimosa. In five minutes follow the small levada as it curves left, away from the track (which continues straight ahead). Five minutes later you pass a narrower levada rushing down to the left (**2h15min**). Then, from a grassy verge, you have a splendid view down to Caniçal and towards the wind generators on São Lourenço Point.

The same view comes into focus 20 minutes later, this time from the far side of the **Ribeira do Serrado** (see below). Three minutes later you can avoid the awkward levada bridge by using the path in the stream bed below (**2h40min**). Soon the fine buttress of rock formed by the **Lombo do Vento** and **Pico Judeu** rises nearby on you right. A red earthen track crosses the levada, and you leave the woods behind.

With more wide-ranging views you soon near the end of the walk. The levada rounds a bend and now the narrow path runs at the top of a concrete wall high above the main road (**3h**). This is a stunning section of the hike. When you come to a concrete track, descend left to a red and white barrier, where you can *flag down* a BUS (**3h15min**). Motorists should turn right and follow the ER109 through the CANIÇAL ROAD TUNNEL (add 15min; there is a pavement).

São Lourenço Point from the levada path in the Ribeira do Serrado

13 PONTA DE SÃO LOURENÇO

Distance: 7km/4.3mi; 3h   **Another photograph page 14**

Grade: moderate, with climbs and descents of about 150m/500ft overall, but only recommended for experienced, sure-footed walkers with a head for heights. The walk would probably be fairly easy if you go with a guided group, but it is potentially hazardous for those unused to 'reading the terrain'.

Equipment: walking boots, long trousers, long-sleeved shirt, sunhat, picnic, water, whistle; cardigans and anorak with hood in cool weather

How to get there and return: 🚌 to/from Abra Bay, where the ER109 ends (Car tour 2). Or 🚐 113: to/from Abra Bay (June-Sept *only*); to/from Prainha (see Timetables and add 2km/35min road-walking each way); to/from Caniçal, then taxi (pay the driver to wait for you).

Short walk: Abra Bay to the viewpoint over the north coast and return. Easy-moderate, but you must be sure-footed on one short stretch; 35 minutes return; *especially recommended* as a leg-stretcher on Car tour 2. Stout shoes, sunhat. Access as main walk. Follow the main walk for 20min, then return to the car park.

The sun-tanned arm of São Lourenço Point beckons you when you first approach the island by air. Whether you're an experienced walker or just a novice, do spend a day out here. Not only are there interesting flora and rock formations to be seen, but you come almost face-to-face with the full fury of the Atlantic thrashing against the coast and offshore rocks. Wear your sunglasses! The colours of the sea and the rocks are dazzling.

Start the walk where the ER109 ends, at tranquil **Abra Bay** (**Baía da Abra**; *P*13). Circle to the right of the knoll, walking below and to the right of the picnic tables. You enjoy

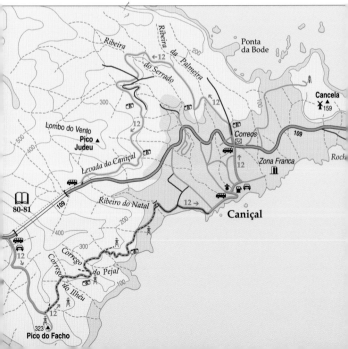

a fine view of the lighthouse at the end of the point, the eyelet in the lighthouse rock, and the Desertas Islands. Notice the lovely strata opposite you, on the far side of Abra Bay. You can also spot your ongoing route: an earthen track heading along the arm of the peninsula, on the south side of a hill with fencing and a triangulation stone. After rounding the knoll, drop down to this track using one of the many paths, then head east. Go through a gap in an old stone wall (**10min**) and then come upon wonderful views (**15min**; *P*13): to the right is Abra Bay and to the left the north coast headlands as far west as São Jorge. Soon, at a fork, go left, coming to a lip of rock on the north coast in half a minute (**20min**). Here you overlook the magnificent 'sea horse' rocks shown on page 14. The colours are astounding: they seem almost fluorescent, so intense is their purple-red colour as they thrust up from a turquoise-to-indigo sea.

Return to the fork and head left, climbing a path and bedrock. *(But for the Short walk, turn right at the fork, back to the car park.)* At a pass (**25min**), the path appears to end … but your ongoing route is visible on the hillside opposite. Look left on the bedrock: you will spot a cairn and some waymarking posts. The path turns 90° left here, straight up the nose of bedrock, and then turns right, above a shallow valley. The path frequently changes level on this stretch, and some scrambling is necessary. *Experienced* walkers will spot the frequent cairns and waymarking posts (although the latter are not concreted in place and may well disappear in storms).

Some **45min** into the hike the character of the walk

Ponta de São Lourenço

Ponta de São Lourenço

changes completely; the path is good, and you might like to take a break at a sheltered, grassy spot.

Seven minutes later (**52min**) you come to a stone marker, 'TC/75' at the **Estreito** (straits). From the marker walk 90° left over bedrock, until you overlook the north side of the point. Then follow the sturdy metal fencing, descending in zigzags back to the main path.

From here on the going is really easy and totally exhilarating. This area has flora under recovery, and you are asked to keep to the paths laid out by the Department of Forestry and Parks. The path passes to the left of the park rangers' house (CASA DO SARDINHA) and continues up to the top of the hill beyond it (**1h35min**). The path ends here: the 'hill' you have climbed is only half a hill; beyond the summit there is simply … an abyss. You're at 150m/500ft — a fantastic vantage point relative to the surrounding terrain. If you can bear to look over the edge, into the abyss, you'll see the rest of the peninsula hanging on by a thread of rock, and the Ilhéu do Farol with its lighthouse; these shreds of land are only accessible from the sea.

It may have been a slog up the hill in full sun, but now you have the joy of running down it. The park rangers at the Casa do Sardinha do not mind a couple of picnickers enjoying a break in the shade of palms, but ask first and *leave no litter*. It's so romantic, you might even be tempted to try Eve's trick and share an apple with your mate. The house was built in the early 1900s by a businessman from Funchal called Sardinha; a little quay (*cais*) for his boat is nearby. Now the forestry rangers use it to bring in their supplies.

From here retrace your route, once again puzzling your way over bedrock. You'll be back at the CAR PARK in **3h**. There is usually a refreshment van here.

14 NORTH COAST PATH: CANIÇAL TUNNEL • BOCA DO RISCO • PORTO DA CRUZ

Distance: 13.5km/8.4mi; 4h10min

Grade: moderate, but you must be sure-footed and have a head for heights (**danger of vertigo**). The path, 350m/1150ft above the sea, is narrow, often slippery, and *prone to landslides* (usually between Boca do Risco and Espigão Amarelo, below Pico Larano). Organised walking tours use this route regularly, and fencing protects the worst stretches (but there is always the possibility that it will be damaged by storms).

Equipment: walking boots, sunhat, long trousers, long-sleeved shirt, picnic, water, whistle, cardigans, anorak with hood

How to get there: 🚌 113 to the Pico do Facho bus stop
To return: 🚌 53 or 78 from Porto da Cruz

Short walk: See Short walk 11 on page 72.

Alternative walk: Larano — Espigão Amarelo — Porto da Cruz. 7.5km/4.7mi; 2h50min. Fairly easy, but you must be sure-footed and have a head for heights (**danger of vertigo**). Equipment, return as above. Access : 🚌 53 or 78 to Porto da Cruz, then taxi to Larano, where the tarred road ends. (🚗: You can also refer to the map overleaf to drive here and walk along the coastal path as long as you like.) At Larano the start of the walk is signalled by a sign with an orange stripe and three stars: follow this track all the way to the coastal path, which you meet above Cova das Pedras. Follow the path to Espigão Amarelo, where there is a stone marker ('JMG'). Or follow it all the way to Boca do Risco, from where you could join Short walk 11. To return to Porto da Cruz from Larano, pick up the notes for the main walk at the 3h20min-point. *NB: see also Alternative walk 15, for a different approach to Larano.*

T his is a walk of contrasts. Amble along the Levada do Caniçal, marvelling at the sun-blessed fertility of Madeira's soil. You can forget for a while what it has cost the islanders in toil, for there are few tiny terraces here, just lush farmland. Then climb from the levada to the crest of the coast. Here the wind wakes you to the cruel realities of life on the island. The north coast between Boca do Risco and

West of Espigão Amarelo your coastal views are framed by pines. Here's where you will see banks of pink belladonna lilies in the autumn.

Porto da Cruz is perhaps the quintessence of Madeira — nowhere else on the island can match its rugged, proud beauty in sunlight; few places in the world could match its harsh anger when lashed by storms.

Begin the walk at the PICO DO FACHO BUS STOP on the west side of the CANIÇAL ROAD TUNNEL. Cross the road and find the **Levada do Caniçal** (see Walk 11) beside the waterhouse. Follow the levada northwest for about **35-40min**, until you come to a path crossing the levada. It leads diagonally up from a house and electricity poles below on the left. Follow the path uphill to the right. The climb is gradual at first, through farmland, where you will likely as not see children carrying huge wicker baskets of fodder on their heads. Later brush and bilberry take over, leading to forests of mimosa and pine. The air is delicious and fresh, with just a hint of salt blowing in from the sea. Within **1h10min** you reach the lip of the coast at **Boca do Risco** (the 'dangerous gap'). Here are houseleeks like great cabbages, snowball trees, thistles, gorse, ferns, laurel, heath and wild flowers in every colour you can imagine. Off across the sea to the northeast, Porto Santo should be clearly visible.

Turn left to make for Porto da Cruz on the narrow path (sign with an orange stripe and two stars). Soon

after passing through a gate, look back east for a view of the Ilhéu do Guincho ('Screech Islet') — so called because the wind shrieks through its tiny eyelet. This is one of our favourite views ... dazzling in morning sun or glimmering in afternoon glow. Then new headlands come into view and, by **2h20min**, you'll reach a promontory with a stone marker ('JMG') just above the **Espigão Amarelo** ('Sharp Yellow Point') ... a splendid lunch spot. As you take a break here, you may be as awe-struck as we are by the fencing the shepherds have built below the path and down the cliffs. Even more baffling is the narrow strip of cultivated terraces in the east, stretching almost all the way from the cliff-top down to the sea at what looks like a 60° angle!

The character of the coastal path changes dramatically beyond the gate at the stone marker, its starkness soon softened by pine forests and, in the autumn, banks of pink belladonna lilies. You look down to a sea of palest turquoise through pine trees standing tall in ochre-red soil. The waves break over the rocks below again and again and again, creating endless patterns of the finest lace. Before long you catch your first views of Porto da Cruz, huddled below Eagle Rock. In the foreground, a dinosaur's back of a ridge thrusts out into the sea.

By this time a track has come underfoot, and at **3h05min** the track leaves the cliff. You descend into a valley with emerald crops and laden vines, where you eventually join an asphalt road (**3h20min**). This is **Larano**. Follow the road downhill. In 10 minutes, it bends sharply left. Straight ahead you'll see a hill with caves. Leave the road here, descending concrete steps to the right. You pass to the left of the caves on a stone-laid path which then takes you down to the sea.

When you reach the mouth of the **Ribeira da Maiata** (**3h45min**), you have several choices. In dry weather, you can wade across the stream at its narrowest point (only a few steps across). Then you can either stone-hop all along the shore to Porto da Cruz or climb the steps on the far side of the river, up to the road (which you follow to the right). In winter, or if there has been heavy rain, you will have to turn left just *before* the river and follow a dirt track for 500m/yds, back to the Larano road. Turn right here, then turn right on the road to Porto da Cruz. From the road you'll have a fine view of your destination, focusing on its rock, old sugar refinery and church. This road takes you into the lower part of **Porto da Cruz** (**4h10min**). The BUS STOP is uphill, on the main ER108, in front of the Centro de Saúde.

15 FROM PORTELA TO PORTO DA CRUZ

Map pages 80-81   **Distance:** 6km/3.7mi; 1h55min

Grade: moderate, with a very steep descent. You must be sure-footed.

Equipment: walking boots, long trousers, sunhat, water

How to get there: 🚌 20, 53 or 78 to Portela

To return: 🚌 53 or 78 from Porto da Cruz

Alternative walk: Portela — Larano — Alternative walk 14. 12.5km/ 7.8mi; 4h50min. Grade, access as above. At the T-junction (1h25min) turn right, cross the bridge over the Maiata River, then take the first road on the left. After about 150m/yds, turn left on a dirt track (just before a school) and follow it along the east side of the river, almost to the beach. Then climb an old stone-laid path on the right, past some caves. Eventually concrete steps take you up to the Larano road: turn left to Larano (2h) and do Alternative walk 14 on page 79.

In the 1800s the *borracheiros* used this trail to transport wine, carried in goatskins on their backs, from Porto da Cruz to the south. Visually stunning in its own right, this walk is an ideal approach to Alternative walk 14.

Begin at **Portela**: head east on the lane skirting the north side of the restaurant 'CASA DA PORTELA'; the tar soon gives way to track (*P*15). After 200m/yds, turn left on an old stone-laid trail. Zigzag steeply down (slippery when wet), enjoying the superb view shown below. When the trail forks, go left, passing a water storage tank on your left. The trail becomes tarred and you meet a crossing road (**40min**). Turn right for about 15m/yds, then swing sharp left down a minor road.

Continue steeply downhill through the strung-out village of **Cruz da Guarda**. When you reach a T-junction by the **Ribeira da Maiata** (**1h25min**), turn left to **Porto da Cruz** (**1h55min**). Or make for Larano (see Alternative walk above).

Strung-out villages straddle the ridges between Portela and Eagle Rock.

16 CRUZ • LEVADA DO CASTELEJO • CRUZ

Map pages 80-81, then 105   **Distance:** 9km/5.6mi; 2h50min
Grade: easy, but you must be sure-footed and have a head for heights; **danger of vertigo** on one very short stretch (*no* protective fencing).
Equipment: walking boots, long trousers, sunhat, picnic, water
How to get there and return: 🚌 53 or 78 to/from Cruz, or 🚗: park at the tiny electricity substation at Cruz (just east of Faial), or as close to it as you can, without blocking the busy ER108.
Alternative walk: Levada Nova — Levada do Castelejo — Cruz. 12km/7.4mi; 3h30min. Grade, equipment, return as above. 🚌 53 or 78 to the Achada turn-off ('ish-**trah**-dah pah-rah Ah-**shah**-dah'). From the bus stop, walk down the main road past the 'Referta' sign as far as the road to Cruz da Guarda on the right. Pick up the Levada Nova here, below the road on the *left,* and follow its sluggish flow towards Penha de Águia, through the pretty, but extraordinarily-named valley of Temte Não Caias ('Hold on; watch you don't fall!'). Some 50min along, cross straight over a cobbled trail to join the main walk (at the 10min-point).

Utter bliss! A fast-flowing levada, still totally unspoilt by groups of walkers … with river pools that have never seen a plastic bag or sardine tin. So far. In just over an hour you move from the cornucopia of cultivation below Penha de Águia into the wilderness of the Ribeiro Frio, with its mimosas and ancient fine-leaved laurels.

Start the walk at **Cruz,** a few paces uphill from the ELECTRICITY SUBSTATION. Almost opposite the 'Cruz' sign there are two roads: climb the old one, on the right, passing a bar/shop on your right immediately. Ignore a road off to the right in five minutes, and keep ahead uphill on cobbles. Within **10min** you come to the **Levada do Castelejo,** on your right. *(The Alternative walk comes in here, from the left.)* Turn right, walking against the current. Lime-green vines will frame your photographs of Penha de Águia, São Roque and Faial.

Beyond a road crossing (**20min**) São Roque's church on the next *lombo* seems close enough to touch. Then you turn sharp left up the magnificent valley of the **Ribeira de São Roque** (*P*16). In **40min** the levada channel is but a ribbon on the escarpment, and there is no protection from the sheer drops. Other drops are encountered further on, but they are all masked by scrub, and the path is always at least 60cm/2ft wide.

In **1h25min** you're at the levada's source; stone steps take you down to the boulder-strewn **Ribeiro Frio.** The pools are so clear that you might be tempted to swim. Only birdsong disturbs the peace of this primeval place.

From here return to **Cruz** (**2h50min**).

Walks 16 and 17 look out over São Roque and across the Metade and Seca valleys to the great peaks.

17 PENHA DE ÁGUIA

Map pages 80-81 **Distance:** 3km/1.9mi; 2h30min

Grade: a strenuous climb of 450m/1475ft and descent of 350m/1150ft. The upward path is diabolically slippery, with grit, loose soil and pine needles underfoot. *Only recommended for very experienced walkers and only advisable in summer,* when local walkers will have hacked a way through the dense foliage. **Danger of vertigo!**

Equipment: walking boots, sunhat, long-sleeved shirt, long trousers, picnic, water, whistle, walking stick; extra cardigans and anorak in cool weather

How to get there: 🚐 53 or 78 to Porto da Cruz, then taxi to the Bar Galé in Penha de Águia de Baixo; or 🚗 to Penha de Águia de Baixo (the turn-off is just east of the São Roque River; Car tour 4); park near the Bar Galé.
To return: 🚐 53 or 78 from Cruz — back to your base, or to the Penha de Águia de Baixo turn-off, from where you can walk back to your car (add 1.1km/20min).

Alternative ascent: At time of writing the descent path (on the south side of the cliff) was less difficult than the ascent. If you prefer to climb and descend the same way, then take 🚐 53 or 78 to Cruz (or 🚗; park as for Walk 16 opposite). Some 20m/yds below (east of) the sub-station, cross the road and walk up a lane. After just a few metres/yards, turn right in front of a house, on a very narrow path, with a narrow levada on your left. After bending into the valley, in a couple of minutes, a small banana grove pops up on your right. The climb begins just at the end of this tiny grove, on your left (faded splodge of vermilion paint on a tree). Once on the top, climb left for 10 minutes to the triangulation stone. Return the same way. Grade and equipment as above.

When we first did this hike, we were torn to shreds by the most impenetrable jungle of lacerating ferns, gorse and blackberries we'd ever encountered. The secret is to do it in summer or early autumn, after the holiday season has started for the young Madeiran walkers. Unless they precede you with their machetes, you won't even *find* the uphill path, let alone enjoy the views! Since this hike is only recommended for *very experienced walkers,* we have not described the zigs and zags in detail.

Start out at **Penha de Águia de Baixo**: climb concrete steps on the right-hand side of the BAR GALÉ (you pass under its sign). At a Y-fork (**2min**), bear left towards a *palheiro*, passing it three minutes later. There is a fine view back to Faial from here. Beyond the cow-house the narrow path turns left towards the sea. You stumble through blackberries and over broken stretches of path. Sometimes you will lose the path as it crosses bedrock. *Always keep an eye open for unexpected zigzags and aim for the 'dip' between the two 'summits' above.* The path climbs the right-hand side of a densely-wooded ravine which opens out 300m/1000ft above the sea in a small waterfall (hidden from view).

In **55min** you reach the top of the rock's western ridge at a fork: to the right are views down to the sea; ahead is an abyss. Go left, following the ridge and skirting the valley below on the left. Five minutes later you are just above the road to Penha de Águia de Baixo, and this is the best part of the walk. The path, coated with pine needles, is wide and almost level, and there are superb views below on the right, focusing on São Roque and the Metade and Seca valleys, with the high peaks as a backdrop.

Beyond this lovely 'user-friendly' section comes the most unpleasant part of the walk. Even if young Madeirans have hacked out the path for you, you will need all fours to haul yourself steeply up over broken tree roots. It seems neverending, but you finally stagger up to the trig point at the top of **Penha de Águia** (589m/1930ft) in **1h30min**. Now, whenever you are on the north coast, you can look up to this tall white pillar and say with justifiable satisfaction: *I did it!*

Continue along the lip of the mountainside, past the pillar. In seven minutes you will come to a pass (550m/1800ft) and a rock outcrop on the right. The path descending from here is far better than the ascent route. Zigzag down, sometimes through pines, for about 50 minutes. You will eventually drop down to a narrow levada; turn right along it. On coming to houses, turn left down to the ER108 at **Cruz** (**2h30min**). There is a bar opposite. Flag down a Funchal bus at the ELECTRICITY SUB-STATION (no *paragem* sign) or, if you have left your car at the start of the walk, catch a Faial-bound bus opposite the sub-station and ask the conductor for '**Pain**-yah day **Ah**-gee-ah, **Bar** Gah-**lay**'. Alight at the bridge over the São Roque River and climb the road back to your car (add 20 minutes).

18 SANTANA • SÃO JORGE • VIGIA

Photograph page 29   **Distance:** 10.5km/6.5mi; 3h30min

Grade: moderate-strenuous, with over 400m/1300ft of descents and corresponding ascents. *Not recommended in damp weather, when the trails would be slippery, or in strong winds.*

Equipment: walking boots, raingear, anorak, cardigans, long trousers, whistle, sunhat, picnic, water

How to get there: 🚌 103 or 138 to Santana. Ask for '**Vail**-yoh So-**lahr**' (the old *solar*); the stop is 1.7km northwest of Santana's town hall/taxi rank (150m north of Bragados Pub), 400m south of the Quinta do Furão road. By 🚗: park in São Jorge and take 🚌 103 or 138 to the start. *To return:* 🚌 103 from the Vigia turn-off at São Jorge; *be there at least 10min before departure time from São Jorge.*

Shorter walk: Santana — São Jorge. 7.5km/4.7mi; 2h37min. Grade, equipment, access/return as above. End the walk at São Jorge's church.

An old zigzag trail, high cliffs, the throbbing sea beside you … this walk was made in heaven. And if you're heartbroken when it ends, just turn to page 133 — you can do it all again, on the opposite side of the island!

To start the walk, climb the cobbled road on the north side of the 'SOLAR' BUS STOP, passing flower-filled gardens. In **4min** you come to a rosy-pink *solar,* one of the island's early manors, now in ruins. Fork right in front of the entrance, curving below the building on a cobbled trail, overlooking the **Achada do Gramacho**, a small plain laced with vines. On reaching a tarred road at the QUINTA DO FURÃO, turn left and walk up 10m/yds, to where 'Stop' is written on the road, then turn right. Follow the road for some 700m/0.5mi; it skirts to the west of a conical hill, the **Cabeço da Vigia**. Just before you reach the highest point in the road, where there is a stand of pines on the right, go left down an earthen track. Soon the old cobbled trail shown on page 29 is visible beneath the iron-rich soil.

You've begun the exhilarating descent into the **Ribeira de São Jorge**. The setting is magnificent: the great peaks rise inland while, ahead of you, São Jorge's church and lighthouse glimmer brightly above a blue, blue sea. On the far side of the valley, you can see your path up to São Jorge; it begins by some cottages snuggled amidst tiny banana groves. Another path skirts the coast.

All too soon the descent ends; at **1h** you're crossing the old bridge. Turn right and follow the coastal path, past a shop/bar on the left and a beautifully-kept house beside the banana groves. Just beyond it are the few remains of **Calhau**, once such an important port that it boasted both a church *and* a chapel! Part of an old wall, with remnants of tiles, still rises near the sea. Opposite the first of the ruins is a tap and the path we'll climb later to São Jorge. The wide sea-side path takes you deliciously close to the pounding breakers.

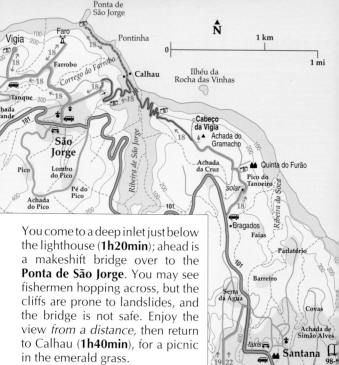

You come to a deep inlet just below the lighthouse (**1h20min**); ahead is a makeshift bridge over to the **Ponta de São Jorge**. You may see fishermen hopping across, but the cliffs are prone to landslides, and the bridge is not safe. Enjoy the view *from a distance,* then return to Calhau (**1h40min**), for a picnic in the emerald grass.

From Calhau turn up the steep trail by the tap. As you climb, look across to your descending path, etched into the cliff on the far side of the river. By **2h15min** you will have huffed and puffed up to a junction. Cross half-left over the road and climb cobbled steps towards the cream-coloured walls of São Jorge's cemetery. Facing the cemetery gate (**2h25min**), turn right up a road, after seven minutes passing a chapel on the left. Continue round left to visit the magnificent baroque church in the centre of **São Jorge** (**2h37min**). Nearby are a bar and a BUS STOP. *(The Shorter walk ends here.)*

Walk back to the palm-shaded chapel and turn left. Ignore a road off right; continue ahead along the ESTRADA MUNICIPAL DO FARROBO. Beyond a stream (**Corrego do Farrobo**), climb to a T-junction and turn right to visit the LIGHTHOUSE (**3h**). Then return to the *estrada municipal* and turn right. At a three-way junction turn right to the **Vigia**, a viewpoint reached five minutes later (**3h25min**). From here the views west capture the attention, especially over Ponta Delgada's seaside church on a flat spit of land, with Cabanas above and Ribeira da Janela in the distance. Now return to the Estrada Municipal do Farrobo (**3h30min**) — you can flag down a bus at the VIGIA SIGNPOST. (It's a good idea to arrive 10 minutes early, to be on the safe side!)

19 PICO DO ARIEIRO • PICO RUIVO • ACHADA DO TEIXEIRA

Map on reverse of touring map; see also photographs pages 4, 93

Distance: 6km/3.7mi; 3h10min

Grade: very strenuous, with steep ascents (about 550m/1800ft overall) and descents (about 700m/2300ft overall). You must be sure-footed and have a head for heights; **danger of vertigo**. Five tunnels en route (20min total). *Sometimes the walk is impassable due to landslides.*

Equipment: walking boots, raingear, anorak, cardigans, long trousers, whistle, sunhat, picnic, plastic bottle/water purifying tablets, torch, walking stick

How to get there and return: ⛴ taxi to Pico do Arieiro and back from the Achada do Teixeira (or with friends who are touring; Car tour 4)

Short walk: Pico do Arieiro — first or second viewpoint — Pico do Arieiro. 35min-1h15min. Stout shoes, sunhat. Moderate ups and downs on hundreds of steps; you must be sure-footed and fairly agile; **possibility of vertigo**. Access/return: ⛴ car or taxi to Pico do Arieiro.

Alternative walks

1 Pico do Arieiro — Pico Ruivo via the Torres. 10km/6.2mi; 4h30min. Grade as main walk, but ascents and descents of about 750m/2500ft overall. One 100m-long tunnel. Although this route is waymarked and mostly protected with fencing, these slopes are prone to landslides. Unless you are a very confident hiker, used to 'exposure', consider doing this walk with an organised group. Follow the main walk through Pico do Gato (45min), then fork right through the gate. After a short downward stretch, the *real* climbing begins, over hundreds of badly-worn steps. It takes almost an hour to reach the pass on the eastern shoulder of the Torres (1800m/5900ft; 1h45min). Beyond the pass, the path curves left and descends in zigzags and more steps. Finally (2h35min) you come to a junction, where the fifth (final) tunnel of the main route is on your left. Pick up the main walk just after the 1h15min-point.

2 Pico do Arieiro — Pico Ruivo — Queimadas — Santana. 16km/10mi; 6h. *Only possible in after a long period of dry weather.* Equipment and access as main walk; add another 1200m/3900ft of steep descent. A route for masochistic experts! Do the main walk, then cross the car park at the Achada. Go to the front of the building and walk past it. Below you will spot the basaltic dyke shown on page 93, Homem em Pé. Descend to the right of it and continue down to the road not far below. Follow the road a short way downhill to a viewpoint, from where the path continues (at the left side). *From here on the very steep clay path can be as slippery as ice.* Hang on to heath trees where you can, and take a walking stick! Some 1h20min from the Achada, go through a gate and soon reach the upper house in the story-book setting of Queimadas Park. From the lower house (1h30min) take the steep cobbled road down to Santana (allow 1h30min). Turn right on the main road: buses leave from the town hall (the building with a clock).

3 Pico do Arieiro — Pico Ruivo — Torrinhas — Curral. 13.5km/8.4mi; 6h15min. Add another 1000m/3300ft of steep descent. Do the main walk and, at Pico Ruivo, pick up Alternative walk 20 on page 92.

Try to make a *very* early morning start and get to Pico do Arieiro at daybreak. The sun erupts like a ball of fire; shards of light cascade mauve and golden over mountaintops and valleys. The mists clear quickly but reluctantly,

Do start out as early as possible. This photograph was taken at about 10.30, just below Pico do Arieiro. The mists are already descending, obscuring the first viewpoint (to the right) and the Torres peaks behind it. Pico do Cidrão is the attractive red wedge on the left, at the head of the Cidrão and Metade ravines. Built in the late 1960s, Madeira's most famous mountain path is very well engineered, and the difficult stretches are protected by sturdy wire fencing. It sometimes come down in storms, but this route is now so popular that repairs are made fairly quickly. If you are unlucky enough to walk just after a landslide, **please use good judgement and turn back.**

curling lovingly around the peaks, mere wisps and whispers and then they're gone. A shepherd appears suddenly from beneath a crest, shouldering a heavy load of firewood, sending goats and sheep scurrying between light and shade, as fluffy clouds throw shadows across the scrubby slopes.

The photograph at the top of page 108 gives you a good overview of the ups and downs of your route. Here on Madeira's third highest peak (1818m/5965ft), you are far above the great Cidrão and Metade ravines. Most mornings the air is so clear that you can see to the heights above Porto Moniz.

Start the walk at **Pico do Arieiro**: follow the paved path shown above. You cross a very narrow spine — a foretaste of the great chasms to follow on this trail linking the island's three highest mountains. The ups and downs begin almost at once, as you struggle over a massive knoll protruding from the spine and then descend to a grassy verge (**P**19), a fine picnic spot. In **15min** you reach the first viewpoint along the route, from where there is a good view down to Fajã da Nogueira, setting for Walk 24. From here you can also discern, to the northwest, a path around the east side of the **Torres**, the island's second highest mountain (Alternative walk 1). The jagged teeth crowning this 'Peak of the Towers' hide Ruivo from view for most of the walk. But you *can* see the island's highest peak — and, on a clear day, the outskirts

90

of Funchal — from the second viewpoint, reached in **25min**.

In **30min** a steep descent on yet more steps begins; at the end of this descent, a ROCK ARCH will frame your photographs. Follow the path through the arch and soon look right to get splendid views over the Metade Valley and the village of São Roque perched on its *lombo.*

A FIRST TUNNEL is met in **45min**; it passes through the isolated needle of **Pico do Gato** ('Cat's Peak'). Beyond this tunnel, a gate on the right leads to Alternative walk 1; keep *left* here. (This short stretch, the scene of a massive landslide in 1996, is potentially the most hazardous and was only reopened in 1999.) Then go on into the second tunnel (**1h**). The third and fourth tunnels follow on immediately. Just past the fourth, a grassy, broom-bedecked knoll commands spectacular views to Pico Grande and the Paúl da Serra.

Enter the FIFTH AND LAST TUNNEL in **1h15min**. At its exit, the Torres path comes in from the right. The ongoing path to Pico Ruivo now skirts a cliff-edge with some caves. Soon the way is very like the trail between Ruivo and Encumeada: the broom gives way to gnarled heath trees which grace sweeping vistas over the Metade.

It's a tiresome slog up to the Ruivo REST HOUSE (under **2h**), where you may be able to buy a drink. After tackling the SUMMIT OF **Pico Ruivo** (**2h10min**), follow the paved path from the rest house down to the **Achada do Teixeira** (**3h10min**).

20 ACHADA DO TEIXEIRA • PICO RUIVO • TORRINHAS • ENCUMEADA

Map on reverse of touring map   **Distance:** 18km/11.2mi; 6h25min

Grade: very strenuous, with overall ascents of 550m/1800ft and descents of 1100m/3600ft. You must be sure-footed and have a head for heights: there is *no protective fencing* at the (very few) exposed points; **danger of vertigo.** *Avoid the walk in wet weather, when the hundreds of stone steps are slippery.* Expect to be caught up in mists. We have never encountered landslides en route, but don't discount the possibility. You must walk quickly, too; bus times are very tight! ***Important note:*** Several paths radiate north and south from this walk, but only the routes described are used regularly. *Experts* may wish to tackle some of the others (which we mention in passing), but we would not recommend any of them and so have not highlighted them in colour on our map.

Equipment: walking boots, raingear, anorak, cardigans, long trousers, whistle, compass, sunhat, picnic, plastic bottle/water purifying tablets, walking stick

How to get there: 🚌 103 or 138 to Santana or 🚌 53, 78 or 103 to Faial, then taxi to the Achada do Teixeira. You will have to walk faster than our times to catch 🚌 6! Consider staying overnight in Santana, to give you time to *savour* this walk; you might even start at sunrise, as we do (arrange this with a taxi in advance).
To return: 🚌 6 from Encumeada (or telephone from the bar at Encumeada for a Ribeira Brava taxi and take a later bus from Ribeira Brava)

Short walk: Achada do Teixeira — Pico Ruivo — Achada do Teixeira. 5.5km/3.4mi; 1h50min. Moderate climb and descent of 270m/900ft on a stone-paved path (with shelters and springs en route). Stout shoes, cardigan, anorak, sunhat, picnic, water. Access: as above (ask the taxi driver to wait for you or to return for you), or by 🚗 (Car tour 4).

Alternative walk: Achada do Teixeira — Pico Ruivo — Torrinhas — Curral. 16km/10mi; 5-6h. Access, equipment, grade as above (but a further 400m/1300ft of very steep descent, on a path often covered with slippery eucalyptus leaves). Do the main walk and, at Torrinhas Pass, descend the path waymarked in red and yellow flashes. You reach the bridge over the Ribeira do Curral 1h45min below Torrinhas; this is Fajã dos Cardos. Follow the road to the right for 20min, to Cumial (just over 5h), where you can catch 🚌 81, or climb up to Curral (6h; 🚌 81).

Blood red, then mauve; and finally silver and blue and gold. All was shadow; all was light. Nothing was real. Where sky ended and sea began, where mountains soared and clouds tiptoed down — all was merged into one. Sunrise at Pico Ruivo, the ideal time to start this walk.

Start out at the **Achada do Teixeira** (*P*20). First walk behind the house to admire the view shown opposite, then turn west on the paved path to Pico Ruivo; you'll pass some springs and shelters on the way. About **40min** up, you enjoy wonderful views of Arieiro, the Torres and the path of Walk 19. The path from Arieiro comes in from the left, and you quickly reach the government REST HOUSE below Pico Ruivo (**45min**; refreshments sometimes available).

Five minutes above the house, you'll come to a saddle and a sign indicating that this path was built in 1949 and that it is 16km from here to Encumeada. At the left are steps to the summit of **Pico Ruivo** (1862m/6105ft; **55min**), with its twin viewpoints. You'll want to linger up here to see how many landmarks you can spot, including the Pico das Torres, Torrinhas Pass, Pico Grande, the Paúl da Serra, the Metade and Curral valleys, and the *pousadas* at Queimadas. To the northeast Porto Santo floats like a cloud on the horizon.

From the summit, return to the signpost and turn down left for Encumeada. The path is well waymarked with red and yellow flashes. Twenty minutes below the saddle, reach a first gate. The path continues through the gate, but first climb up slightly to the right, to see the fantastic views over the north coast, about 1300m/4250ft below. Beyond the gate the valley leading down to Curral das Freiras opens up before you almost at once, and you can see the higher hamlet of Fajã dos Cardos (near the end of the Alternative walk).

In **1h40min** come to a particularly good viewpoint over Curral's setting; now the path dips down south for a while, before resuming its westerly course. In **1h55min** start climbing to skirt a cone-shaped sandstone peak on your right ... all the while enjoying the perfume of wild mint and thyme crushed underfoot.

At **2h05min** you'll reach a promontory with chasms to the left. Here, a disused path to Curral via Lombo Grande goes straight ahead; we go to the right. At **2h25min** climb down some steps and into another valley, from where you can again see the north coast. You may also spot another derelict path, this one leading down right to São Jorge via Pico Canário, just before Pico das Eirinhas. Already you can see across the great valleys of the Ribeira Brava and São Vicente rivers,

Homem em Pé ('Man on Foot'), an impressive basaltic dyke just below the Achada do Teixeira house. From here there is a fine view down over the São Jorge Valley (Picnic 20; Alternative walk 19-1).

which split the island in two, and the pronounced hairpins of the road from Feiteiras to the Paúl da Serra. The path squiggles endlessly, alternately giving views over the north and south of the island.

In **2h45min**, find a perfect promontory for lunch. Here two or three people can sit wedged in nature's rock-chairs and picnic overlooking Curral das Freiras. This is just before you reach a fork (where there *may* still be a large painted stone). Here a clear path descends left to Curral, but this is *not* the path we recommend for the Alternative walk. We head up *right* here. Not far beyond a gate, the path descends about a dozen steep and slippery stone steps beside a precipice; ***there is no protection.*** *Stow everything away before you make this potentially dangerous descent!* Then reach a grassy verge overlooking the north coast — an ideal picnic spot for groups of walkers.

Soon you are confronted by the first of *many* flights of steep stone steps. These lead up to **Torrinhas Pass (3h)**, where signs point the way to Curral, Pico Ruivo, and Encumeada. *(The Alternative route descends to the left here.)* You may also see a sign pointing to the threadbare remains of the old (1800s) trail to Boaventura; it too, is derelict, and its lower reaches have succumbed to the asphalt of the ER108. The path now takes you over the shoulders of **Pico do Jorge** — forever up and forever down — a climb and descent of over 200m/650ft lasting almost an hour, on giant-sized steps.

Beyond a signposted SPRING on the left (**4h30min**; not far before a shepherds' fireplace), a rock arch frames your photographs of the valleys of Serra de Água and São Vicente. Then descend through a glen of giant ferns beside a basalt escarpment at **Pico do Ferreiro**. At **4h55min** you may see an arrow pointing to a steep path down left: part of a 1800s trail connecting this path with the Jardim da Serra via Pico Grande, it is heavily broken by landslides.

This part of the walk, west of Pico do Jorge, can be glorious. But mists frequently descend by early afternoon, obscuring the valleys. Mist will be a boon for those who suffer from vertigo: the hundreds *and hundreds* of STONE STEPS on which you descend 300m/1000ft to the end of the walk seem to spiral in space, but in heavy mist the abyss is not apparent, and all you can see are the many nearby *folhados* (wild lily of the valley trees). Fortunately the steps are amply wide!

Eventually a steep dirt track takes you to the ER228 at **Encumeada** (1004m/3293ft; **6h25min**). Walk 31 can begin here, at the *miradouro* over the São Vicente Valley. Follow the road south over the pass, to find the SIGN TO FOLHADAL beside the **Levada do Norte**, starting point for Walk 32. Wait here for the BUS, or telephone for a taxi from the bar.

21 PICO DAS PEDRAS • COVA DA RODA • CRUZINHAS

Map pages 98-99   **Distance:** 8.5km/5.3mi; 2h35min

Grade: easy-moderate ups and downs, with a descent of 600m/1950ft and an ascent of 180m/590ft at the end of the walk

Equipment: stout shoes (walking boots preferable), long trousers, anorak, sunhat, cardigans, picnic, water

How to get there: 🚌 53 or 78 to Faial or 🚌 103 or 138 to Faial or Santana, then taxi to the Rancho Pico das Pedras on the ER218
To return: 🚌 103 or 138 from Cruzinhas

Short walk: Pico das Pedras — Queimadas — Pico das Pedras. 4km/ 2.5mi; 1h10min. Easy. Stout lace-up shoes with good grip (the path can be *very* slippery), picnic, water. Access/return: 🚗 car or taxi to/from the Rancho Pico das Pedras on the ER218, where the Levada do Caldeirão Verde crosses the road (Car tour 4). Walk through the 'ranch', with the chalets to your left and the restaurant to the right; the levada continues on the far side of the buildings.

Alternative walk: Queimadas — Caldeirão Verde — Cruzinhas. 23km/ 14.3mi; 6h30min. Grade, equipment, access: see Walk 22, page 97. Do Walk 22 first. On returning to Queimadas from the Caldeirão Verde, follow the levada to the crossing of the ER218 at the Rancho Pico das Pedras. Then do the walk described below. Return on 🚌 103 from Cruzinhas.

This walk is at its best in summer or early autumn, when the hydrangeas bordering the levada are bursting with melon-sized blossoms and the tiny terraces in the valleys are aglow with golden hayricks.

Start the walk at the RANCHO PICO DAS PEDRAS, 250m/yds below the Pico das Pedras forestry house. The **Levada do Caldeirão Verde** crosses the ER218 here. Follow the blue and yellow sign, heading southeast for Faial (or, for the Short walk, go west towards Queimadas). Stroll beside the levada under the shade of holm oaks, eucalyptus and a 'forest' of cornflower-blue hydrangeas. After **10min** turn left down a track, with the levada beside you on your left. Five minutes later, turn down left again; don't follow the narrow levada

Hydrangeas flank the start of the walk, near the Rancho Pico das Pedras

The steep terracing in the Ribeira Seca near Cruzinhas is at its most colourful in summer.

ahead — the path is too overgrown. In **20min** a track comes in from behind you and to the right: ignore it. Five minutes later, ignore another track off to the right. In **30min** you pass a lone house on the left. Keep ahead downhill for 400m/yds, to a crossroads (**35min**), where a tree stands in the middle. This is **Cova da Roda**. A track goes left to Santana, and the one we have been descending continues ahead to Faial, immediately passing a water tank on the left. Turn down *sharp right* here.

As you descend, look out left for an old stone-laid trail on the far side of the **Ribeira da Abelheira**, and for the path down to it. (If you miss this path, your track will end at a small tunnel bored for water exploration; just retrace your steps for about 200m/yds to find the path, on your *right*.) You descend to a STONE BRIDGE (**45min**). Ten minutes later you have splendid views of 'Eagle Rock', before dropping down into the Lombo do Galego Valley.

Pass through **Lombo do Galego**, and ignore a road off left: instead, turn sharp right, keeping to the old trail. A second stone bridge is met not far downhill, just beyond a WATERFALL (**1h30min**). Continue towards the next valley, pausing to admire the majesty of Penha de Águia in front of you.

Another glen introduces a THIRD BRIDGE (**1h55min**), and a further descent takes you to a fourth bridge at **Fajã da Murta**. Soon tar comes underfoot and you cross the **Ribeira Seca** (**2h05min**), one of the three great rivers flowing to Faial. Once over this fifth bridge, watch for concrete steps on the left which take you back to the old trail. From here it's a 30-minute climb; you cross the road once more before reaching **Cruzinhas** and the ER103 (**2h35min**). There is a large BUS SHELTER nearby.

22 QUEIMADAS • LEVADA DO CALDEIRÃO VERDE • SANTANA

Distance: 18km/11.2mi; 5h15min

Grade: moderate, but you must be sure-footed and have a head for heights. The levada path is very slippery and broken away in places. **Danger of vertigo** throughout (very severe drops on one side, adequately protected by fences, *but these often come down in storms*). Four tunnels (10min total). Steep descent to Santana.

Equipment: walking boots, torch, long trousers, cardigans, anorak, whistle, picnic, plastic bottle/water purifying tablets, walking stick

How to get there and return: 🚌 103 or 138 or 🚗 to/from Santana, from where you can take a taxi to Queimadas to begin the walk.

Short walks: Levada do Caldeirão Verde. Follow the main walk as long as you like; return the same way. Or follow the levada east to the Rancho Pico das Pedras (Short walk 21 in reverse). Take a picnic and cardigans, and *wear lace-up shoes with very good grip; when damp, the red clay soil here is like a skating rink!* Be sure to ask the taxi driver to return for you. 🚗: Travelling by car, see the notes for Car tour 4 on pages 27-28: you may prefer to park at the Rancho Pico das Pedras on the ER218.

T hink green. Think of rain forests … of emeralds. This is Queimadas — a mossy paradise. Take advantage of the 10-minute break in the bus journey at Poiso or Ribeiro Frio and fortify yourself with a warm drink or a 'Madeiran breakfast' (a glass of sweet Madeira wine and a warm hard-boiled egg). This will set you up for the drop in temperature on the descent to the north coast — where as much as 2m/80in of rain can fall in a year!

When you arrive at **Queimadas Park** (*P*22), you will find two charming *pousadas*. **Begin the walk** by passing the lower houses, to discover yet another *pousada* — this one a miniature for the muscovy ducks who live in the pools. Cross the wooden bridge and follow the wide path beside the old

The Levada do Caldeirão Verde (Walks 22, 23 and 28) is densely-wooded with heath trees and laurels, creating a lovely play of light and shade. Heath tree branches are used all over Madeira for fencing. Their gnarled curves make a pretty picture, straight out of a story book.

Ilha de São Jorge

Levada Nova

Ribeira de Sebastião

Ribeira de São Jorge

Ribeira Bonita

Gamal
Lombada
do Meio
Er
28

Sítio do
Terreiro

Achad
do Marqu
28

posto florestal

Ribeira dos Arcos

Pico Alto
846

Vale da Lapa ▲
981

Ribeira dos Cedros

28

22, 23

Levada dos Tornos

22, 23
22, 23

Levada do Caldeirão Verde

28

Queimadas

21

P

Ribeira Grande

21

21

19

Ribeira

Ribeira da Fonte do Louro

Calderão
Verde

Ribeira de Silveira

Calderão
do Inferno

Levada do Pico Ruivo

23

23

23

23

□ 144

Achada do
Teixeira

19

Levada do Caldeirão Verde. The red clay underfoot is *diabolically slippery* — walk on moss where you can. In **13min** pass through a gate, beyond which the path narrows. Four minutes later, be sure to leave the levada where it is broken away — the paths down and back up are slippery too.

The views are spectacular as you follow the levada westwards to one of the most remote parts of the island. After crossing two ravines — the **Ribeira dos Cedros** (**27min**) and the **Ribeira da Fonte do Louro** (**45min**) — you come in about **1h** to the first, very short TUNNEL. Two minutes beyond the exit, ignore a path off right signposted to Ilha. (*Walk 28 leaves us here.*) Immediately you plunge into the second tunnel (five minutes). There is a path on the right at this tunnel exit, too, but we found it wasn't viable. The third tunnel lies just beyond this path; it's very low: *keep your head down* for the next two minutes. Not far past this third tunnel, you must leave the levada again to avoid an overhanging precipice.

Go through a final, very short tunnel in a couple of minutes and, 13 minutes later (**1h35min**), come to a spillway and a sluice. Climb up the path at the left of the spillway to see the lovely 300m/1000ft-high falls and pool, the **Caldeirão Verde** ('Green Cauldron'). Then continue on the levada. In a few minutes (**1h45min**) you will come to our favourite picnic spot — a promontory in the sun overlooking the **Ribeira Grande**, some 500m/1650ft below.

From here allow 3h30min to descend to **Santana** via the Queimadas road. Turn right on the ER101; the bus leaves from the TOWN HALL (the building with a clock; **5h15min**).

23 QUEIMADAS • CALDEIRÃO DO INFERNO • QUEIMADAS

Map pages 98-99   **Distance:** 15.5km/9.6mi; just over 5h
Grade: as Walk 22, page 97. But because the section between Caldeirão Verde and Caldeirão do Inferno is *prone to landslides and not protected by fences*, we recommend this walk for experts only.
Equipment: walking boots, long trousers, plastic rainhat, cardigans, waterproof anorak or raingear, whistle, picnic, plastic bottle/water purifying tablets, torch, walking stick
How to get there and return: 🚗 car or taxi to/from Queimadas (or the Rancho Pico das Pedras: see Short walk 21, page 95). If travelling by bus, see Walk 22, page 97, and add 1h30min to walk down to Santana.
Alternative walk: Queimadas — Caldeirão do Inferno — Pico Ruivo tunnel — Fajã da Nogueira — ER103. 20km/12.4mi; 6h40min. Map continues on reverse of touring map. Grade, equipment, bus or taxi access as main walk. In addition to the hazards of the main walk, you must pass through a tunnel 2.4km/1.5mi long. *Each member of the party must carry a good torch.* Follow the main walk to the Caldeirão do Inferno. Then return to the Pico Ruivo tunnel (20min). Plunge in. You exit about 40min later by booming waterfalls and clear pools, where the Ribeira Seca, coming down from its source on the Pico das Torres, crashes into the levada. Another tunnel (12min to pass) lurks beyond this one. After these, the final few tunnels are a doddle. The levada is soon covered by a jeep track. About 1h30min from entering the Ruivo tunnel take the track down left to the power station (1h; Walk 24b ascends this track). From the power station walk on for 1h15min to the ER103 (🚌 103).

T he awe-inspiring chasm of the Caldeirão do Inferno is hidden below the eastern flanks of Pico Canário and the northern escarpment of Ruivo — about as close to the heart of primeval Madeira as you can get. As always, the levada builders have been there before you, taming the wilderness and opening your path.

   The walk begins at **Queimadas**. Use the notes for Walk

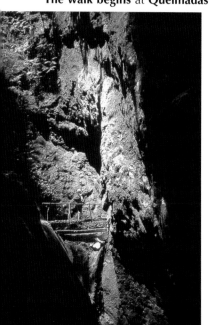

Water for the Levada dos Tornos is captured at three main sources (described in Walk 24, page 102); the Caldeirão do Inferno is just one of them. Left: crossing the Ribeira Grande, on the approach to the 'Inferno' ('Hell's Cauldron'). Right: at the source. Don't expect to see roaring waterfalls here; this is just surface water, pouring down from Pico Canário (1591m/5220ft). What is magnificent is the escarpment rising 300m/ 1000ft above you — at its most impressive after rain.

22, page 97, as far as the sunny promontory overlooking the valley of the Ribeira Grande (**1h45min**). Should you decide to have lunch here, you can have some fun with the aptly-named swifts! If you toss some bread into the air, these acrobatic birds will catch it in mid-flight.

Then continue along the levada. Another impassable section of levada is encountered in **2h**: slither down to the right and scramble back up again. In **2h05min** come to steps up to the left (the levada takes its source not far ahead, in a beautiful setting with a waterfall). These steps are easily climbed, but coming down it's another story — a descent into nothingness, with no protective fencing.

You ascend 80m/260ft to a newer levada, the **Levada do Pico Ruivo**, at 960m/3150ft (**2h13min**). Ahead of you are two tunnels. To the left is a short tunnel (no torch needed) opening onto more fine views. The 2.4km/1.5mi-long Pico Ruivo tunnel has old railway tracks dating from its excavation. Steps also continue uphill here (we think they lead to the Pico Ruivo path from Ilha mentioned in Walk 28, but have not had time to investigate). To the right is a large WATER TANK. Skirt the edge of the tank (there is cable fencing). Just beyond the tank you have to walk under a waterfall and will no doubt get soaked. Immediately afterwards, go through a first short TUNNEL. Three more follow. Then you come to roaring waterfalls in a cavern at the head of the **Ribeira Grande** (**2h27min**). This chasm is crossed via two very NARROW BRIDGES (see opposite) or, in dry weather, you can descend to the river bed below. Beyond here you pass through four more short tunnels (the first one *appears* to be blocked off — the opening is just a narrow gap at the right-hand side). You come to

the setting shown here — the **Caldeirão do Inferno** (**2h32min**), source of the Levada do Pico Ruivo.

Dwarfed by this escarpment lies a tiny levada channel — just a trickle in a grassy sun-trap. It's so still you can hear the trees breathing. Relax at this magnificent picnic spot before returning to **Queimadas** (just over **5h**) … or going on to the nearby valley of Fajã da Nogueira via the Pico Ruivo tunnel (Alternative walk).

Map: reverse of touring map   **Distance:** see Walks a and b below

Grade: both suggestions are easy-moderate, with a climb/descent of 400m/1300ft on tracks. (The initial climb is tedious in the extreme, but you will find it well worth the effort!)

Equipment: stout shoes, long trousers, sunhat, cardigans, anorak, picnic, water, torch, walking stick

How to get there and return: 🚗 car or taxi to the power station at Fajã da Nogueira. (The walks are also accessible by 🚌 103 or 138 to the turn-off for the power station; add a soul-destroying 4.5km each way.)

Walk a: Pico da Nogueira. 7km/4.4mi; 2h30min. **Walk b: Ribeira Seca.** 11km/6.8mi; 3h40min. These routes diverge at the 40min-point.

Alternative walk: Levada do Pico Ruivo and Levada da Serra. 14km/8.7mi; 5h45min. *A more satisfying walk than either a or b above, but only recommended for sure-footed walkers with a head for heights; **danger of vertigo**. At time of writing this path was adequately protected by cable fencing, but it may well come down in storms. Equipment as above, but wear walking boots; take a whistle and plastic bottle/water purifying tablets. Follow Walk b to the Ribeira Seca and back. Continue* past *the track you ascended. Walk with the flow of the Levada do Pico Ruivo (and later the Levada da Serra) for 1h25min, until you come to a tunnel (4h). Just inside it is the underground water tank (it was not possible to build this large reservoir on the open mountainside). Descend the track in front of the tunnel and, less than 10min downhill (just before a keepers' house), turn right uphill at a T-junction. You reach the top of the pipe on Pico da Nogueira, outside the tank (35min from the tunnel). To return to the power station, go down the track and, at the fork before the keepers' house, continue down the main track. In 15min (5h) ford the Ribeira da Fajã da Nogueira (or cross it on a makeshift bridge). You meet your outgoing track 10min later, just above the clearing with the enormous* tils. *The power station is 35min downhill.*

T he Levada dos Tornos (Walk 7) was born here in the wilderness of Fajã da Nogueira in 1971, when the power station was inaugurated. Water for the Tornos is captured at three main sources. One lies far to the northwest: an extremely long tunnel carries water from the Pôrco and São Jorge rivers directly to this power station. Another conduit is the rebuilt Levada da Serra do Faial e Juncal, which runs from the Juncal River to an underground reservoir and then a pipe on Pico da Nogueira. The third source is the Caldeirão do Inferno (Walk 23): its waters flow through the Pico Ruivo tunnel to the same pipe, whence both levadas plummet down to the power station.

All the walks begin at **Fajã da Nogueira**. Climb the jeep track at the right of the POWER STATION. In **20min** you have superb views of the Torres ahead and Pico da Nogueira, with its pipe, on your left. In **35min** Pico do Arieiro is just ahead; the Miradouro do Juncal is also prominent. Pass a clearing on the left, with two enormous fire-ravaged *til* trees. (During this walk you will see some of the oldest laurels on the island, with trunks over 8ft in diameter.) Two minutes past the clearing (**40min**), a track joins from the left.

Walk a turns left down this track, in 10 minutes fording the **Ribeira da Fajã da Nogueira** (or crossing on a makeshift bridge). Continue uphill for about 20 minutes, to a fork near the keepers' house, where you ignore the track to the right. In **1h20min** you come to the top of the pipe, outside the underground reservoir. Nearby is a grassy verge, perfect for picnicking. From here you overlook the sinuous Ribeira do Juncal and the Metade Valley. You're at 960m/3150ft; not far below, you can see an old levada that used to run between Balcões and Fajã da Nogueira, now completely crumbled away. Return the same way (**2h30min**); from the keepers' house, you could take a detour up left (20min return) to see the levada and underground reservoir.

Walk b keeps ahead, climbing to the **Levada do Pico Ruivo** (covered by a track; **1h10min**). Turn right, walking against the water's flow and coming to the setting shown below left. Past two keepers' houses and some short tunnels, at **1h40min** you enter a TUNNEL WITH RAILWAY TRACKS (12 minutes). You'll hear the roar of waterfalls on the far side before you exit high up in the **Ribeira Seca** (**1h52min**), by crashing falls and clear pools — a superb picnic spot. From here the PICO RUIVO TUNNEL leads to Walk 23, but we turn back to the POWER STATION (**3h40min**).

Left, Walk b: At 1h10min the Cabeço da Fajã dos Vinháticos is just in front of you; its velvety emerald ridges ripple down the north side of the Ribeira Seca. Right: The Alternative walk edges the Levada da Serra between the two tracks. Better fencing was built in the late 1990s.

25 LEVADA DO FURADO: RIBEIRO FRIO • LAMACEIROS • PORTELA

See also photographs pages 2, 108   Distance: 11km/6.8mi; 3h25min

Grade: moderate, but you must be sure-footed and have a head for heights (**danger of vertigo**). The most precipitous sections of the levada are well protected with iron railings, *but there are several exposed stretches without fencing.*

Equipment: walking boots or stout shoes that grip on slippery surfaces, long trousers, anorak, sunhat, cardigans, plastic bottle/water purifying tablets, picnic, whistle

How to get there: 🚌 103 or 138 to Ribeiro Frio
To return: 🚌 20, 53 or 78 from Portela

Short walk: Ribeiro Frio — Balcões — Ribeiro Frio. 2km/1.3mi; 40min. Easy; 🚌 103 or 138 or 🚗 to/from Ribeiro Frio. The signposted path is below the souvenir shop. Follow it beside the dry levada; in 20 minutes you'll pass through a cut in the towering, moss-covered basalt and find yourself high in the Metade Valley. Soon come to a fork, where the old levada goes left; turn right and you're at the Balcões (***P***25) in a minute. Superb views over Fajã da Nogueira and to the great peaks.

Alternative walks: grade, equipment, access as main walk

1   Ribeiro Frio — Ribeira do Poço do Bezerro — Chão das Feiteiras — Ribeiro Frio. 7km/4.3mi; 2h50min. Ascent of 300m/1000ft; equipment as main walk; *map page 107.* A five-star walk, *but not suitable in heavy mist!* 🚌 or 🚗 to/from Ribeiro Frio. Follow the main walk to the 1h-point, then clamber up to the path on the embankment above the left-hand levada channel. Follow this narrow levada to its source in the Ribeira do Poço do Bezerro (2h; lovely pools). From here retrace your steps for a minute, then turn left up a narrow path. The path takes you up to a plateau (the Chão das Feiteiras; 2h15min). Head straight across, through ferns *(feiteiras),* aiming for the right-hand side of the col ahead. In 10 minutes, three houses appear ahead and to the right. Turn right on the grassy track in front of them but, after 200m/yds, curve left on a grassy trail. Soon cobbles come underfoot. Descend to the ER103, cross it, and pick up the continuing trail 200m/yds downhill. This beautiful old trail emerges just above the trout hatchery (2h50min).

2   Ribeiro Frio — Lamaceiros — Levada da Serra. You can join the Levada da Serra at the Lamaceiros waterhouse and continue for as long as you like: see Walk 10, page 70.

3   Ribeiro Frio — Pico do Suna — Portela. 13.5km/8.4mi; 4h20min. Follow the main walk for 2h10min. Just before the tunnel, climb the good path on the left; some 20min up it widens to a track. When you meet a crossing trail, turn left up to the fire tower at Pico do Suna (30min; see Walk 26). Return the same way and continue to Portela.

This is a walk to which we return again and again, to enjoy the wonderful play of light and shade along the levada, the frisson of excitement at the Cabeço Furado, and the spectacular views in the second half of the walk.

   Begin the walk just below 'VICTOR'S' bar/restaurant at **Ribeiro Frio.** Here you will see a SIGNPOST TO PORTELA on your right (further downhill, on the left, is the sign for Balcões; ***P***25). Here you join the fast-flowing **Levada do Furado.** In **20min** pass a tunnel on the right, with a waterfall. In **1h**, just by a bridge over the **Ribeira do Poço do Bezerro**, two fast-flowing levadas course down into the main channel at a grassy verge — a splendid picnic spot. *(Alternative walk 1 climbs the embankment here.)* The finches here have been tamed by 'Landscapers' (see photograph on page 2), and will expect to be fed some titbits! About eight minutes beyond this bridge **keep careful watch** for the first of many deviations from the levada; often it is far easier *and safer* to cross the shallow stream beds rather than follow the channel.

In **1h20min** you pass through a massive cleft in the rock, where stepping stones bridge the channel — a good challenge for photographers. Soon there are splendid views

Anyone can follow the levada for just a short way, to revel in the play of light and shade over rocks and waterfalls, laurel and heath trees. The second part of the walk, beyond the Lamaceiros waterhouse, is completely different. You cross sunny pastures, enjoying panoramas of majestic mountains, proud valleys, and the tranquillity of the north coast villages in the distance.

to the high peaks, especially the jagged crown of the Torres (photograph page 108). At **2h** a strong path off to the left leads to a fine view over São Roque and Faial after only a minute. At about **2h10min** you will pass through a very short tunnel. Just before it, a path on the left doubles back over the levada and climbs to Pico do Suna *(Alternative walk 3)*. Two minutes later you come to a precipice, where the very narrow levada path is cut into the Suna escarpment at the **Cabeço Furado**. This excitement lasts for 10 minutes.

By **2h35min** you'll reach the peaceful setting of the **Lamaceiros** waterhouse and look out east to São Lourenço. *(From here you can go on to the Levada da Serra; Alternative walk 2; there is also another path up to Pico do Suna.)* About 30m/yds past the waterhouse, turn left down a path to find the narrow **Levada da Portela**. Follow it to a forestry house (with picnic tables and toilets), and here join a track at the right. Descend gently, with marvellous views of Faial, Penha de Águia and Porto da Cruz. When the levada disappears, stay on the track. After 130m/yds, go left on a grassy path to find the levada on your left and pastures on your right. At a fork, head right, following the levada (now on your right).

You'll come to a derelict waterhouse. Go left here: slippery earthen steps edged with lilies and hydrangeas take you down to the ER102. Walk 150m left downhill, pass the 'PORTELA' sign, then turn left on the *Machico* road to the bar 'PORTELA A VISTA' (**3h25min**), where the BUS stops opposite.

26 PICO DO SUNA

Distance: 6.5km/4mi; 2h

Grade: easy descent and ascent of 150m/500ft. *Almost no shade.*

Equipment: stout shoes, sunhat, cardigan, picnic, water

How to get there and return: 🚐 to a parking place on the ER202, 4.2km east of Poiso and 3.6km west of the Sítio das Quatro Estradas, where a track crosses the road diagonally. Or 🚌 103 or 138 to Poiso, walk downhill to the starting point and, at the end of the walk, walk downhill to the Sítio das Quatro Estradas for 🚌 77 (add 7.8km/4.8mi; under 2h).

Alternative walk: Poiso — Pico do Suna — Portela (13km/8mi; 4h) **or Ribeiro Frio** (15.5km/9.6mi; 5h). Grade, equipment: as Walk 25, page 105. 🚌 to Poiso. Follow the ER202 east from Poiso for 4.2km, then do the walk below. Leaving Pico do Suna, turn sharp right downhill when you return to the fork below the peak. This becomes a good path which crosses over the tunnel at the 2h10min point in Walk 25. Watch for the levada as you descend and take one of two paths down to it. Follow it east to Portela (🚌 20, 53, 78) or west to Ribeiro Frio (🚌 103, 138).

Not *all* of the island's best walks are tough. And just to prove it, here's a 5-star, easy ramble suitable for everyone. You 'climb' *down* to your very own peak and, when you've reached it, you look straight down on the summit of Penha de Águia with its tall white trig point. If you have binoculars, perhaps you will spot some exhausted hikers up there. At the end of the day, they can say, 'I've done it!' (on Walk 17 the struggle is 95 per cent of the satisfaction). When *you* get home, you can rest smug in the knowledge that, with hardly any effort, *you were higher than they were and you had an even better view!*

From the flower-strewn slopes near Pico do Suna, you look out west to the high peaks (Walk 19). At the left is the pousada at Arieiro, followed by the isolated 'needle' of Pico do Gato, the jagged Torres, Pico Ruivo and, far right, the Achada do Teixeira.

Begin the walk on the ER202, at the PARKING PLACE described above, where the track crosses the road. Head north on this track. Although it doesn't look very appealing at the outset, in a trice it reverts to an old grassy trail. You're high on the moorlands of Poiso, with only sheep for company. At first the trail contours, and you look over right, beyond the dump *(Vazadouro)*, to Santo da Serra and its reservoir.

In **15min**, just before the trail descends, look for a very narrow path on the left and take it. It will keep you contouring half-left, towards some pine-covered peaks. In **23min**, at a pass, you enjoy the fine view shown above. Ahead is a ladder stile, which you climb over two minutes later. The path continues along the ridge, the **Lombo Comprido**, to a stone inscribed '220', from where you look towards São Lourenço, the *lagoa* at Santo da Serra and the 'Santana'-style houses of the big holiday centre at Quatro Estradas ... as well as the enormous piggery on the Levada da Serra (Walk 10-4).

From here return the way you came for 100m/yds. Then, on the saddle, cut half-left down the hillside on the spongy grass, to rejoin the trail (**40min**). Follow it downhill to the left. Ignore a rough track off right (**50min**) but, when you come to a Y-fork (**1h**) bear right to climb to the fire watchtower on **Pico do Suna** (**1h04min**). What a view! From left to right you scan São Roque, Faial, Penha de Águia, the off-shore rock at Porto da Cruz, Cruz da Guarda, São Lourenço Point, Pico do Facho, and the Machico Valley.

From here follow the trail all the way back to the PARKING PLACE (**2h**).

Walk 27: Levada de Cima, above Boaventura

27 CIRCUIT ABOVE BOAVENTURA

Photograph opposite (below)

Distance: 9.5km/6mi; 3h10min

Grade: easy-moderate ups and downs, after an initial ascent of 100m/ 330ft. But you must be sure-footed and agile, and have a head for heights (**danger of vertigo** on a couple of very short stretches along the levada).

Note: As we went to press, the beautiful old path in the Moinhos Valley (from the 25min- to the 1h-point) had been deluged by landslides from a track being built about 10m/30ft higher up. Once the track (or road) is finished, the path will no doubt be abandoned forever. There are, however, many permutations of this walk: you can follow the track (as described) or use the No 6 or 132 bus or your car to do *parts* of the walk (see bus and car symbols on the map).

Equipment: walking boots, sunhat, water, picnic; extra cardigans and anorak in cool weather, optional swimwear in summer

How to get there and return: 🚌 6, 103, 132 or 🚗 to/from Boaventura

Short walk: Boaventura — Eirinha — Boaventura. 3km/2mi; 1h15min. Easy, but you must be agile. Stout shoes, sunhat, water. Access/return as above. Follow the main walk for 40min, then look down to the right, to spot a lone house with a satellite dish. This house stands on the concrete steps down to Eirinha. A good path leads from the track down to this house; if you don't spot it, ask someone working on the terraces. Once at the house, descend to a road. Catch bus No 6 or 132 here or turn right and walk down to Boaventura (1h15min). Another option is to carry on as far as Roçada and follow the track (or new road) out to the Achada do Castanheiro road; catch the No 6 or 132 bus there or walk down to Boaventura.

The most bucolic and flower-filled walk imaginable, this short hike takes you through magnificent cultivation alternating with jungle-like wilderness, across rock pools where you can swim, and finally along an ancient free-form levada.

Start the walk at the CHURCH in **Boaventura**. Walk along the ER101 towards Santana and, when you come to the telephone kiosk just east of the church, climb the concrete steps opposite it; there is a sign here, 'ORIGEM LEVADA'. You follow electricity wires up a *lombo,* through a tight cluster of houses abounding with flowers. The path levels out in the midst of a profusion of sunflowers and vines.

In **25min** the concrete runs out. At this point, look for a track on your right (under construction at time of writing) and follow it to the right (southwest). The track runs about 10m/30ft above a beautiful old path that rounds the upper Moinhos Valley. While you may catch sight of the path and scramble down to it (as we did), eventually you will no doubt find your way blocked by rubble and you will have to find a way back up to the track.

The track takes you above **Eirinha** in about **40min**. *(The Short walk descends here.)* It eventually drops down to the **Ribeira dos Moinhos** at **Roçada (1h)**. Just before the track crosses the river, turn left on a *footpath*, crossing the river on a concrete bridge. On the far side, turn left on a wide path in a beautiful grassy setting. By some river pools you cross back over to the other side of the river and follow a good stone-laid path.

In **1h15min**, *before* the terraces on the far side of the valley give way to trees, take the narrow path on the right (signposted 'Poço Salão') down to the river pools (the way ahead goes to Falca). Beyond the pools, your ongoing path lies slightly to the right. At a fork a minute uphill, climb steeply to the left. In three minutes you come to the **Levada de Cima**. Its source (*madre*) is less than five minutes to the left.

From the source, turn back and follow the levada north, passing some paths down to the right. Like many old levadas, this one is not always corseted in concrete; it flows quickly and freely — sometimes shallow, sometimes deep ... through cultivation, under chestnuts, below dramatic cliffs. A short vertiginous stretch is encountered in **1h45min**. Note that the levada has been dropping slightly. In less than **2h** you've entered a beautiful wilderness reminiscent of the Castelejo Levada in the Ribeiro Frio (Walk 16). Ignore two paths down right in the next several minutes. The second path is followed by an extremely vertiginous patch, where you may have to wade in the levada for half a minute. Two minutes later, at just over **2h05min**, you pass first house of **Levada de Cima**.

In **2h15min** concrete steps at the far side of a lone house descend to a road in front of a microwave station. Press on: in a minute you enjoy fine views west, past Seixal and as far as Ribeira da Janela. Five minutes later the levada drops over the cliff and into a tank; from here you overlook Ponta Delgada (but not its seaside church or pool).

Return to the concrete steps above the microwave station, descend to the road, and turn right. Yellow lines indicate the No 6 bus stop. If none is due, follow the road back to **Boaventura (3h10min)** — a beautiful stroll overlooking the church and palm-shaded cemetery, dwarfed by a 'sugar-loaf' cliff with an old zigzag trail.

28 QUEIMADAS • VALE DA LAPA • ILHA DE SÃO JORGE

Map pages 98-99; photographs pages 39 and 97

Distance: 8.5km/5.3mi; 3h15min

Grade: moderate-strenuous, with a descent of 550m/1800ft on a very steep and slippery path; you must be sure-footed, and this walk is not recommended after heavy rain.

Equipment: walking boots, long trousers, sunhat, cardigans, anorak, picnic, plastic bottle/water purifying tablets, walking stick

How to get there: 🚌 103 or 138 to Santana, then taxi to Queimadas
To return: 🚌 103 from Ilha de São Jorge

Alternative walk: Queimadas — Vale da Lapa — Queimadas. 10km/6.2mi; 3h05min. Quite easy. Access/return: 🚗 car or taxi to/from Queimadas (or the Rancho Pico das Pedras: see Short walk 21, page 95). Follow the main walk to the 1h25min-point, visit the tiny forestry house, then return the same way.

Two walks in one: on this excursion you enjoy the shady meanderings of the Levada do Caldeirão Verde, and then you leave it for the sunny heights above São Jorge, with views of the north coast villages round to Santana.
  Begin at **Queimadas**: follow WALK 22 for **1h**, when you pass through a very short tunnel (you won't need a torch). Two minutes beyond the tunnel exit, take the path off right (signposted 'Vale da Lapa'). In 20m/yds ignore the path sharp left signposted to Pico Ruivo and continue ahead (signposted 'Ilha'). The path is now waymarked with yellow and red flashes all the way to your destination. You walk along what was once a beautiful stone-edged levada planted with hydrangeas, but the channel has since been filled in with soil. You have fine views to the right over the Levada do Caldeirão Verde and a lower levada in the same valley — the **Ribeira dos Arcos**.
  In 20 minutes there is a signposted short detour left to a 'Fonte' (spring). You then reach a GATE (**1h25min**), just beyond which a path comes in sharply from the left — from the **Vale da Lapa** forestry house. (Allow an extra 15 minutes return if you want to make a detour to this isolated *posto florestal*.) The main walk keeps ahead here, descending a very steep and slippery jungle-like stream bed.
  When you meet a track at a T-junction (20 minutes from the gate; **1h45min**), follow it downhill. At a bend to the right, leave the track and walk ahead past a signpost pointing back to Pico Ruivo. Descending in a gully, cross a track and follow the sign for 'Ilha'. Always keep ahead over ensuing track crossings. When you come to a fork, ignore the right turn to 'Lombada do Meio'; head left for 'Granel' (the lower part of Ilha, near the church, but usually spelled 'Garnal'). The BUS STOP is by the church and bar in **Ilha** (**3h**).

29 LEVADA DA FAJÃ DO RODRIGUES

Photographs pages 19, 31 **Distance:** 5km/3mi; 1h50min
Grade: easy climb/descent of 120m/400ft; the levada path is slippery
Equipment: stout lace-up shoes, sunhat, walking stick
How to get there and return: 🚌 to/from Miradouro (on the ER208 from Feiteiras (Car tours 1, 5). The road is 3.6km uphill from the bridge at São Vicente or 8.3km downhill from Encumeada. When you turn off, *take km readings!* Go straight over a crossroads and left at two T-junctions (0.9km and 2.4km). At 3km (in Miradouro) look left to locate concrete steps with a white arrow and then (at 3.1km) a stony path with street lights. This is where the walk starts; park nearby. Or drive another 400m uphill and turn left on a track. Park near a construction company, saving 90m/300ft of climb and descent (50min walking time).

Here's a short stroll with a marvellous finish, especially included for motorists based at São Vicente. It takes you to a primeval setting almost on your doorstep — a *caldeirão*, or high rock basin streaming with water.

Start out at **Miradouro**. Climb the stony path with street lights. Rise to a crossing track, where there is a construction company on the left, and continue uphill, now on a track. Beyond a large water tank, you meet the **Levada da Fajã do Rodrigues** (**30min**). Turn right on the levada, beside tired apple orchards and a waterhouse with a brightly-tiled table. In **35min** you pass a keepers' house below in the trees. Here you cross both the ER208 and remnants of an old trail.

Threading your way below eucalyptus and beside hydrangeas (photograph page 31), in under **50min** you're at the head of a first valley at **Fajã da Ama**. Five minutes later you come into a very deep valley, where the laurel-coated pinnacles of the **Furna da Areia** tower above you. After crossing two small stream beds on a 'roller-coaster' path covered in pumice, you reach the 'cauldron' (**1h**), where a narrow waterfall drops 200m/650ft. (The levada below it, too dangerous to follow, takes its source 2km northwest in the Ribeira do Inferno; much of it flows through tunnels.)

Return the same way to **Miradouro** (**1h50min**)*, enjoying the view shown on page 19, where the slender tower of Nossa Senhora de Fátima rises on a hillock below in the valley.

*If you have time, first pursue the levada in the other direction for up to 30 minutes; the 'banks' have been newly planted and, 10 minutes from the tank, there is a picnic table on a sunny promontory.

30 LOMBADA DA PONTA DO SOL • LEVADA NOVA • TABUA • RIBEIRA BRAVA

Map pages 114-115; photograph page 34

Distance: 15km/9.3mi; 3h50min

Grade: moderate-strenuous, with a very steep descent of 400m/1300ft at the end of the walk. You must be sure-footed and have a head for heights (**danger of vertigo** on the levada).

Equipment: stout shoes or walking boots, long trousers, sunhat, picnic, water, walking stick; extra cardigan and anorak in cool weather

How to get there: 🚌 4, 107 or 142 to Formiga (Fohr-**mee**-gah; it means 'ant'!) on the ER222, 2.1km east of the turn-off to Ponta do Sol
To return: 🚌 any suitable bus from Ribeira Brava

Alternative walk: Lombada's levadas. Distance optional; equipment as above. Access: 🚌 as above or 🚗 to Lombada; same transport to return. Two levadas take their source high on the eastern flanks of the Ribeira da Ponta do Sol; *both are vertiginous, the old one* **extremely** *so.* You could explore the old Levada do Moinho for a short time (see text below), then return and follow the main walk to the Levada Nova. Pursue this new levada *to the left,* up the valley, for as long as you like, then return and follow the main walk — perhaps to the Ribeira da Caixa and back.

The enormous rose-pink *solar* at Lombada was for centuries the largest country house on Madeira. And it stood in the largest private estate — the Lombada dos Esmeraldos, stretching from the Paúl da Serra down to the sea between the Ponta do Sol and Caixa valleys. This huge domain had been given by Zarco to one of his sons, who cultivated sugar cane with great success. It was later bought by João de Esmeraldo, a friend of Christopher Columbus. At one time 80 slaves worked in Esmeraldo's plantations and mills; with the wealth created, he built the mansion and nearby church of the Espírito Santo. There is little evidence of the sugar plantations today, but the valleys are still a tapestry of cultivation.

Start out at **Formiga**: climb the road to **Lombada** (see map; **20min**). Look at the old *solar*, then enjoy the superb view over the **Ribeira da Ponta do Sol** (photograph page 34) from the balcony walkway behind the church. Here an iron gate leads to the old (1400s) **Levada do Moinho**; it powered the mills in the sugar plantations. To reach the new levada, start back out of Lombada the way you came in, then take the first left, up a flight of concrete steps (vines are on the left, bananas on the right). You climb 90m/300ft, reaching the **Levada Nova** by a road (**35min**). Turn right here. *(But for the Alternative walk, turn left).*

Now begin to pace out Esmeraldo's domain. You cross the road immediately. Five minutes later, weave between houses, then descend steps to a very narrow road, with a building opposite. Go straight over this road, following another road just to the right of the building (a shop). Walk past all the houses below this road; then, after 150m/yds (after the fifth lamppost), by a gap in the roadside retaining wall, descend concrete steps back to the levada (you reach it by a fig tree and shed). In winter and spring calla lilies and yellow-blooming vetch are a perfect foil for the dark rods of sugar cane still cultivated here (probably for the spirit, *aguardente*). After crossing a concrete path you come into the **Ribeira da Caixa**. The cane peters out as you leave Esmeraldo's ridge, to be replaced by willow, the odd banana grove, and all the ingredients for a hearty vegetable soup. The lime-green grass here is *so* inviting for a picnic. As you near the head of the valley, *watch out for a diversion path below the levada,* as the main path can be very slippery and dangerous in winter. In dry conditions however the main path is more fun: not long after you crouch down through a very short tunnel, you may get drenched by an icy waterfall.

In **1h15min** you leave the valley, coming to a road. Cross over and continue on the levada. Only a minute later a concrete lane crosses the levada; follow this lane 20m/yds downhill to the right, then rejoin the channel (with street lights) on the left. Now head north into the **Ribeira da Tabua**, graced with white iris, broom and sugar cane in spring, hayricks, sweet chestnuts and blackberries in autumn. Beyond a sugar cane grove, in inland **Tabua**, you cross a bridge and then ford a spillway (**2h05min**; or cross a bridge 20m/yds upstream). Heading southeast, then cross the village road on steps. After passing through a cut in the basalt cliffs (**2h15min**), where stepping stones bridge the levada, you enjoy the best views of this valley — its river pools, poplars and hayricks. But along here the path is very vertiginous.

A short tunnel (**2h20min**) takes you into a new valley, and beyond a road, you pass a grassy knoll on the right overlooking coastal Tabua. In under **2h45min** the levada disappears beneath a walkway. Turn left up concrete steps, to **Corujeira**, where a road descends to the ER222. Follow the road downhill to the right for 50m/yds, to where the levada continues on a high parapet. This is so vertiginous that it is easier to walk down the road: keep left at the junction quickly encountered. Just past the junction, the road makes a U-bend in the **Ribeira da Caldeira**. Here take the *second* set of steps on your right, to descend to the levada. You meet a narrow concrete road (**3h**): turn right and join Walk 31 just after its 4h35min-point, dropping steeply to **Ribeira Brava** (**3h50min**). The BUS STOP is on the seafront esplanade.

31 ENCUMEADA • LEVADA DO LOMBO DO MOURO • RIBEIRA BRAVA

Map begins on the reverse of the touring map and ends below

Distance: 15.5km/9.6mi; 5h25min

Grade: strenuous, with a climb of 300m/985ft to start (but see 'How to get there' below) and a very steep descent of 1300m/4265ft. You must be sure-footed and have a head for heights (**danger of vertigo**). Two major (but stable) screes to be crossed at the start of the levada.

Equipment: walking boots, long trousers, sunhat, cardigans, anorak, picnic, plastic bottle/water purifying tablets, whistle, walking stick

How to get there: 🚌 6 to Encumeada Pass (*not* the Residencial Encumeada), or 🚕 taxi from Ribeira Brava or São Vicente to the Lombo do Mouro signpost on the ER110 (deduct just over 4km/1h30min).
To return: 🚌 any suitable bus from Ribeira Brava

The Lombo do Mouro, a dinosaur's back of a ridge, is the setting for a delightful levada walk … but save it until you've acquired your 'Madeira knees' — the descent to Ribeira Brava will leave them quaking!

Start out at **Encumeada**: walk to the north side of the pass and climb the ER110 to the **Lombo do Mouro** signpost, on

The descent to Ribeira Brava (left); the rushing levada and the Lombo do Mouro house, below the escarpment of the Paúl da Serra (Picnic 31)

your left after just over 4km (**1h30min**). Walk down to the beautifully-sited government rest house and hunting lodge (**1h40min**; **P**31), where you join the **Levada do Lombo do Mouro**. Follow its flow; you cross two screes before moving away from the detritus of the ER110. There are fine views east towards Pico Grande (Walk 4), Achada da Pinta (Walk 5) and the Arieiro/Ruivo trail (Walk 19; photograph page 119). Go through a gate in **2h10min** and then perhaps take a break in the tall golden grass — a delightful picnic spot, with orange butterflies pursuing the purple thistles and foxgloves, and the levada surging down beside you.

In **2h40min** you come into the eucalyptus zone, so you know that you have already dropped to below 900m/3000ft. Five minutes later the levada describes a wide arc and descends very steeply (photograph above). In the east the pine forest at Boa Morte (Walk 6) makes a pleasant picture.

From time to time you will be aware of a track sidling up to the levada and eventually you're forced to join it. It takes you to a road (**3h55min**). Turn left for 250m/yds, then go right, down a steep concrete lane. When you join another road, follow it downhill for 400m/yds, then go left on concrete. From here on, always take the steepest route downhill, with the dramatic **Brava Valley** close by on your left. At **4h35min** cross straight over another asphalt road; 60m/yds further down, Walk 30 comes in from the right, just in front of a garage. Beyond a stretch of concrete steps, turn left at a T-junction (**4h45min**). At another T-junction (**4h55min**), keep left down more concrete steps. When you meet the ER222, go left downhill and find the final flight of steps down into **Ribeira Brava** (**5h25min**) — where you can collapse in a café. The BUS STOP is on the seafront esplanade.

32 FOLHADAL AND THE NORTE AND RABAÇAS LEVADAS

Map on reverse of touring map   **Distance:** 8.5km/5.3mi; 2h50min

Grade: easy, but you must be sure-footed and have a head for heights (**danger of vertigo** on the Levada das Rabaças). Two tunnels (one fairly long).

Equipment: stout shoes, good torch *for each member of the party*, sunhat, plastic bottle/water purifying tablets, picnic, cardigan, anorak

How to get there and return: 🚌 6 or 139 to Encumeada pass (*not the* Residencial Encumeada); 🚌 6 to return. Or by 🚗: park at the viewpoint on the north side of the pass (Car tours 1, 5, 6).

Short walk: Encumeada — Folhadal — Encumeada. 4km/2.5mi; 1h. Equipment, access/return as above. Follow the main walk to Folhadal and back. *A 5-star walk on a fine day; the paths are amply wide, and there is little danger of vertigo, but good torches are essential.*

Alternative walk: Encumeada — Cascalho — Encumeada. 16.5km/ 10.2mi; 5h. *Expert:* very narrow levada paths, many of them unprotected (**danger of vertigo**), and at least two potentially hazardous screes; one very long tunnel. Access/return, equipment as above (but wear walking boots and long trousers and take a whistle). This is an alternative approach to the *caldeirão* (rock basin pouring with waterfalls) visited in Walk 36. Follow the main walk for 2h, then go through the long tunnel (30min). Follow the levada into the Ponta do Sol Valley. Cascalho ('scree') is the source of the Rabaças Levada (3h; see notes page 126). Return the same way.

Power and majesty. These may be your first impressions when you step onto the levada at Encumeada Pass. You are at the centre of the deep north/south cleft that splits the island. The great peaks rise in the east; the magnificent valley of Serra de Água lies to the south. And at your feet, the Levada do Norte, 1.5m/5ft deep and just as wide, surges along in a massive concrete channel. You're bound for Folhadal, a primeval wonderland of ferns and ancient laurels.

Left (top and bottom): greenery on the Levada do Norte path to Folhadal. Right: looking east towards Pico Grande from the Levada das Rabaças, just past the tunnel, where the Levada do Norte comes in from Folhadal. (The fog is pouring out of the tunnel!)

Start the walk opposite the bar/restaurant, on the south side of the pass at **Encumeada**, where a sign indicates 'Folhadal'. Climb concrete steps here up to the **Levada do Norte** and follow it westwards, past the keepers' flower-filled house. You'll be amazed by the abundance of vegetation: conifers of every description, heath and hawthorn, with a tangle of laurel, azaleas, lilies, hydrangeas, and myriad wild flowers. If you're walking here in June, you'll see the splendid cornflower-blue 'Pride of Madeira' in all its glory. In **12min** you come to the promontory of **Lapa do Galho** (*P*32): from here you enjoy fine views down over the valley and the south coast. You can also see the levada continuing to the east and emptying into the metal pipe down to the power station (inaugurated in 1953). There are 50km/31mi of channels north of here (including 11km/ 6.8mi of tunnels). From the power station the water flows on in another 35km/22mi of channels (7km/4.5mi of tunnels) to irrigate the terraces of Ribeira Brava and Câmara de Lobos (see Walk 6).

Past the promontory the levada forks (**14min**). Turn right and follow the Levada do Norte into the tunnel, which will take about 10-12 minutes to pass through. We'll never forget our first walk here: we approached the tunnel to find what looked like a washing machine gone mad. Thick white 'foam' was pouring out of it (see photograph on the previous page) — fog, rushing through from the other side!

The tunnel exit (**25min**) frames your first glimpse of **Folhadal**, a 'museum' of ferns and indigenous trees — *vinháticos, tils* (laurels) and white-barked *paus brancos* (olive family). But your eyes will be drawn to the *folhados* for which this wood is named — the autumn-flowering lily of the valley trees, native only to Madeira. Keep ahead through the *laurisilva*, enjoying views to the São Vicente valley — until you come to a second tunnel (**45min**). From here return* the same way to the fork (**1h15min**).

Now turn right to follow the **Levada das Rabaças** (1970), a 'tributary' of the Levada do Norte. It is flowing in from Cascalho, the waterfall basin explored in Walk 36 (and the Alternative walk). In **1h45min** a waterfall on the right heralds a short tunnel (3min to pass). Seven minutes later, you reach a lonely keepers' house above the Pousada dos Vinháticos. In **2h** you come to the long tunnel to Cascalho (*Alternative walk*). Turn back to the 'Folhadal' sign at **Encumeada** (**2h50min**), where the bus stops.

---

*Or first follow the extremely vertiginous levada (no protective fencing) through this and two more tunnels, to a pretty waterhouse on the ER208; allow 2h return (50min in tunnels).

Map on reverse of touring map; see also photograph page 19

Distance: 6.5km/4mi; 2h05min

Grade: easy-moderate, with a descent/re-ascent of about 150m/500ft. You must be sure-footed and have a head for heights to get all the way to Pináculo *(the levada just before 'the Pinnacle' may be **impassable** in winter, when waterfalls inundate the vertiginous, unprotected path.)*

Equipment: walking boots, long trousers, sunhat, cardigans, anorak, picnic, plastic bottle/water purifying tablets, whistle

How to get there and return: 🚌 to/from Bica da Cana (Car tours 5, 6)

Alternative walk: ER110 — Pináculo — Bica da Cana. 5km/3mi; 1h45min. Moderate-strenuous ascent of 400m/1300ft; *not always passable in winter, when the path beyond Pináculo may be inundated by waterfalls and **too dangerous to follow**.* 🚌 Ask friends to drop you off at the sign with the orange stripe and single star on the ER110, 3.3km uphill from Encumeada. Arrange to be collected later by the white and red pillars at the entrance to the Bica da Cana government refuge. From the signpost climb steps up to the Levada do Lombo do Mouro and follow it to the right. Beyond its source, a zigzag path takes you up to the Levada da Serra. Turn right; you will reach Pináculo in 1h. Continue on the levada, *past* signposts for Bica da Cana and Caramujo, and then the levada's source. Under 35min from Pináculo, watch for a blue 'hat' painted on a rock on the ground; here climb a path up to Bica da Cana.

One of our all-time favourite walks, absolutely gorgeous in its own right … and affording a splendid outlook towards the great peaks. You're just on the eastern flanks of the Paúl da Serra, and you'll enjoy the laughter of a vigorous levada and the falls that feed it. This is an ideal, fairly short circuit for motorists.

Start the walk at the red and white concrete pillars at the

Below Bica da Cana, Pináculo rises above heath trees. Fog engulfs São Vicente's valley, but the peaks in the east (Walk 19) are bathed in sun.

ENTRANCE to the **Bica da Cana** REFUGE. Head to the left of them, descending a grassy path through ferns. You skirt to the left of fence posts and the large heath tree grove behind them. In **4min** climb over a stile. Just beyond it, go left at a fork. Continue down beneath a leafy bower. In **12min**, at a T-junction, turn right. (If you look behind you here, you'll see a blue 'hat' painted on a rock.) Now you're on the fairly overgrown and very wet (even in high summer!) path that will take you to Pináculo.

In **30min** you reach the source of the **Levada da Serra**, where wild carrots and *Senecio* spill down the cliff. In **35min** come to a sign, 'Caramujo' (indicating an old farm, now derelict) and a few metres beyond it, an *arrow* indicating Caramujo. Our path back up to Bica starts just opposite this arrow, but for now continue on the levada for eight minutes, when you'll come to our favourite lunch spot: here you can sit in long golden grasses ablaze with foxgloves and butter-flies, beneath waterfalls foaming down a high and mossy basalt rock face (**43min**). A gentle valley lies before you, leading the eye to São Vicente and the chapel of Nossa Senhora de Fátima (photograph page 19). Hawks circle watchfully above. Just past here is the giant basalt **Pináculo** (**45min**). Continue along the levada as long as you like — perhaps for another 15 minutes — just to enjoy the negative ions, the flowers, and the views.

Before you lose height, turn back. Pass 'the Pinnacle' (**1h 20min**) and, on reaching the *arrow* indicating Caramujo, turn left uphill on a good path (**1h30min**). You pass a stone on your right inscribed 'MN' (**1h40min**). A minute later a deep gully is crossed. Turn left on a footpath on the far side of it, making for the heights, where you can see a fence. When you come to the fence, turn right uphill in front of it (there may be a sign here with an orange stripe and one star). Make for the Bica da Cana viewpoint, where two isolated trees stand out as landmarks (even in fog). Some wind generators are behind you, to your left. The fence turns 90° to the left not far below the viewpoint: continue *straight ahead* uphill through ferns, aiming just to the left of the two isolated trees. You can see a fence ahead; turn right just in front of it. After a few yards a stile (or gap; **1h55min**) gives access to the far side of the fence.

Walk to the trig point ahead on a good path through ferns, passing a tiny meterological outpost bristling with gorse. Visit the **Bica da Cana** VIEWPOINT (**P**33), then follow the skiddy pumice track back to your car at the ENTRANCE (**2h05min**).

34 FANAL

Map begins on pages 124-125, continues below; photograph page 8

Distance: 18km/11.2mi; 4h30min

Grade: easy, but danger of thick mists descending (if this happens, do not stray off the track/road).

Equipment: stout shoes (walking boots in wet conditions), sunhat, anorak, cardigans, whistle, picnic, water

How to get there and return: 🚍 (Car tours 5 and 6) or taxi to the Paúl da Serra. Either hire a taxi for a full day, or first take a bus to 'Recta das Canhas' (see Walk 35, page 122) and arrange for the Canhas taxi driver to wait for you or to come back for you in time for your return bus. Ask the driver for 'Caminho do Fanal' (Kah-**mee**-noh doh Fah-**nahl**).

Note: We have kept this walk in the book, even though the surface underfoot is so miserable. The beautiful old trail to the Fanal has been gouged away to make a 'road' that may never be surfaced and is only motorable in high-suspension vehicles. But you can sometimes walk on bits and pieces of old trail at the side of this rubble track; *the Fanal is worth seeing.*

The air will be crystal-clear, the panorama endless; and even with the sun fully up, dew-drops will sparkle on the gold-green grasses of the Paúl. You're bound for the Fanal, where ancient indigenous laurels are now under government protection. Hopefully only seagulls and butterflies will keep you company, not vans or jeeps.

The walk starts on the ER110, by the signpost 'FANAL/ RIBEIRA DA JANELA'. Follow the road; *keep it in sight,* but leave it wherever possible. By **25min** you reach the deep valley of the **Ribeira dos Cedros** on the left (Walk 37 delves into this valley). Five minutes later, on your left, you overlook the red-tiled roofs of the Rabaçal houses and, just above them, the reservoir wall. To the right you can see the north coast.

By about **1h50min** you are drawing near to a cone-shaped mound with trees parading up its left flank — **Pedreira**, landmark of the **Fanal**. Come to a track off right and follow it past the forestry house (**2h05min**). When you're well to the north of Pedreira, climb up the promontory at the right for lunch. From here you look down on the breathtaking beauty of Chão da Ribeira, the Ribeira do Seixal, and the sea.

Return the same way to the JUNCTION on the ER110 (**4h30min**).

35 CAMPO GRANDE • LEVADA DO PAÚL • RABAÇAL • LORETO

Distance: 15km/9.3mi; 4h55min
Grade: moderate, with a slight **possibility of vertigo** on the levada
Equipment: stout shoes (walking boots preferable), sunhat, anorak, cardigans, picnic, plastic bottle/water purifying tablets, strong torch
How to get there: 🚌 107, 115 or 142 to Recta das Canhas ('**Ray**-tah dahs **Kahn**-yahs'), where there is a taxi rank. Ask the driver to take you to Cristo Rei, Campo Grande (**Kreesh**-toh **Ray**, **Kam**-poh **Grahnd**).
To return: 🚌 80, 107, 115 or 142 from Loreto
Short walks

1 Levada do Paúl. Walk as far as you like from Cristo Rei along this levada; perhaps to the caves and back. 5km/3mi; 1h30min. Grade and equipment as above (but no torch needed). Best access is by 🚗 (a detour on Car tours 5 and 6). Note that the path may be very wet!

2 Rabaçal — Loreto. 9km/5.6mi; 3h15min. Grade, equipment, access as main walk. Ask the taxi driver to take you to Rabaçal ('Rah-bah-**sahl**'). Follow the main walk from the Rabaçal houses (the 1h40min-point).

An awe-inspiring landscape, all stillness and solitude. The flanks of the Paúl da Serra stretch out before you, endlessly, under a porcelain-blue sky. Only your own shadow and a few sheep will walk with you on the 'marsh of the mountain range'.

The taxi will deposit you on **Campo Grande**, 9km up the road from Canhas, just below a statue of Christ the King ('CRISTO REI'). Here the ER209 crosses the **Levada do Paúl**: there is a small waterhouse on the right and two concrete markers on the left, as well as a sign with a green stripe and one star. This is one of the island's older levadas, now integrated into the new scheme. Further east it is more accurately called the Levada da Bica da Cana, for it takes its source below Bica da Cana, in the Ribeira da Ponta do Sol (Walk 36).

The blue, blue ribbon of the Levada do Paúl

Begin by walking west (**P**35), following the flow of the levada and looking down over the moors to the lush south coast. The levada is ribboning ahead of you — now silver, now amethyst, always mesmerising. There's a narrow bit of path by a waterfall in about five minutes, but no further obstacles. At **25min** pass a river pool, fed by a waterfall; reach a second in **45min**. Here, caves stretch up into the hills on the right (**P**35) — shelter for animals and shepherds in bad weather. In spring the hillside is golden with gorse, the levada mirrors the sky, and a few baby goats dare to gambol along your path. Cows graze freely on the lower slopes.

At **1h10min** you'll see a large building up to the right (the hotel at Urze), as well as a metal pipe in the distance. The pipe is carrying water from the reservoir above Rabaçal down to the Calheta power station. The turbines of this station (commissioned 1953) feed on water from five separate levadas: you are walking one of them now, Walk 38 introduces a second, and Walk 37 explores the other three. From the power station the water is sent eastwards to irrigate the fields of Calheta (14km/8.7mi of channels) and westwards to Ponta do Pargo (40km/25mi of channels). Walk 41 ambles along this levada, from Raposeira.

Crossing an earthen track, you come to a tiny chapel beside the levada (**1h15min**). The levada continues into the reservoir, from where it is piped down to the power station. Cross the ER110 (Porto Moniz/Encumeada road), where you will see the **Levada da Ribeira Grande** (Walk 38) below the road. Walk left, to a large parking area (usually full of souvenir stalls). Here take the narrow road down towards Rabaçal. After crossing the **Ribeira do Alecrím** with its lovely pools (**1h25min**), continue downhill under the watchful eyes of goats until you arrive at **Rabaçal**, a government rest house (**1h40min**).

When the tarred road ends, turn right down a dirt track to the **Levada do Risco**. Follow the track beside it for five minutes, then fork left down a path, to the **Levada das 25 Fontes**. Turn left when you reach this levada, following the flow (both of these levadas are explored at leisure in Walk 37). Fifteen minutes' walking along this enchanting watercourse will bring you to a grassy sun-trap outside the entrance to the first major tunnel built on Madeira, in the mid 1800s (notice the poignant shrine). It takes under 20 minutes to pass through this very high tunnel, built to accommodate people on horseback. Unfortunately, today we have to share the path with an intrusive shoulder-high water pipe.

Soon you've left the shade of Rabaçal for the sunny heights of Calheta's *lombos,* where you'll find a keepers' cottage, a rustic picnic table and a tap. *Before* you reach the cottage, continue left along the levada for about 50m/yds, until it flows under a rock overhang. Here descend and cross a narrow concrete bridge. Then head downhill to the right on a grassy path, through heath trees, mimosa and pine. In **2h50min** you will meet two pipes carrying water from the tank down to the power station. Five minutes later, a single pipe holds the flow of the levadas of Risco and 25 Fontes. Soon meet the **Levada da Rocha Vermelha** and follow it to a waterhouse and small tank, whence it too shoots down to the power station. (*Alternative walk 37-2 joins here.*)

From here a jeep track takes you to the wide **Levada Calheta–Ponta do Pargo** (**3h25min**). Turn left and enjoy a sunny stroll with views over the south coast. Some 35 minutes along, turn right down any cobbled trail to descend through **Florenças**. Meeting the main ER222 (**4h25min**); turn left and come to **Loreto**'s plane-shaded centre and chapel after **4h55min**. The BUS stops here.

36 CASCALHO

Map begins on pages 124-125; ends on the reverse of the touring map

Distance: 9km/5.6mi; 3h

Grade: moderate, with a descent and re-ascent of 400m/1300ft; you must be sure-footed and have a head for heights (**possibility of vertigo**).

Equipment: stout shoes (walking boots preferable), cardigans, long trousers, sunhat, anorak, picnic, plastic bottle/water purifying tablets, whistle, walking stick, *torch*

How to get there and return: as Walk 35, page 122

Alternative walk: Levada da Bica da Cana. 12.5km/7.8mi; 3h. Fairly easy climb/descent of 100m/330ft, but **possibility of vertigo** on the narrow levada path. Equipment, access/return as main walk. Follow the main walk for 40min, then continue on the levada, to climb to its source just below the Paúl da Serra (1h35min). Return the same way.

Cascalho is a primeval wonderland, known only to goats, levada builders and a very few guides and walkers. It's a hidden bowl of waterfalls where the Ribeira da Ponta do Sol gathers its strength. This torrent now feeds the Levada das Rabaças (Walk 32).

Begin the walk on the ER209 below the statue of 'CRISTO REI': head east on the **Levada da Bica da Cana**, walking against the flow (Walk 35 heads west here). The bright blue ribbon of water takes you past a lone pine and old fireplace on the left (**20min**; *P*36). Three minutes later you cross a beautiful old cobbled trail (this route descends to the ER101 in 9km/6mi; 2h30min). On the far side of the trail the levada path starts to climb. When the climb levels out two minutes later, you enjoy the spectacular view shown below (*P*36) down the **Ribeira da Ponta do Sol**. Below, to the right, you'll spot your track down to Cascalho.

As you continue on the narrow path, you will probably be astounded to see cows and bullocks grazing freely on this extremely precipitous terrain. It is obvious that walkers have not been here in great numbers, so *the safety of this livestock is your responsibility when you walk here: go slowly and very quietly!*

At **40min** you come to the stony crossing track seen from above: turn down right. The descent is quite gradual, but the rubble underfoot is treacherous. Water, which has been pouring down beside the track in gullies, is soon channelled into a levada. At under **1h** you come to a promontory and a WORKMEN'S SHED. From here there is a superb view down over Lombada on a hilltop in the valley, with its rosy *solar* and white chapel (Walk 30). Continue through the short S-shaped TUNNEL at the left of the shed, and **use your torch:** the levada **crosses** the track in the tunnel.

Picnic 36 can overlook the Ribeira da Ponta do Sol

126

*The Alternative walk climbs 100m/330ft to the source of the levada, sometimes on steps. Experienced walkers, **equipped with a compass**, could scramble from the source up the river bed and make their way to Bica da Cana, to be met by friends (see map on reverse of touring map). But for the average walker, who has left a car at Cristo Rei, this would be **exceedingly dangerous**: fog comes down like a curtain! Remember, the levada is your **only** guide back to your car, and it is unlikely that you would be able to find it again.*

Out of the tunnel, you soon reach a huge basin; the well-channelled levada drops here. You could be forgiven for thinking yourself already at Cascalho ... but it is still hidden. Continue downhill with the levada, past a sluice, tunnel and water pit (**1h15min**). Some cable fencing allays feelings of vertigo now. This is a most exhilarating part of the walk, beside the rushing water. Finally, at **1h20min**, you round another bend and you're finally there — **Cascalho**, the *caldeirão* at the head of the Ribeira da Ponta do Sol, is just ahead of you, with its waterfalls and sluices. Chances are that you'll be enveloped in mist by midday, but in summer the bowl is a suntrap — an exquisite picnic spot.

Allow up to 1h40min (**3h**) to return to the ER209.

37 RABAÇAL'S LEVADAS

Map pages 124-125; see also cover photograph

Distance: 12.5km/7.8mi; 3h45min

Grade: moderate, with a **possibility of vertigo** on the levadas

Equipment: stout shoes (walking boots preferable), cardigans, long trousers, sunhat, anorak, whistle, rainhat, picnic, plastic bottle/water purifying tablets

How to get there and return: 🚗 car or taxi to Rabaçal (Car tours 5, 6). *Note: The road down to Rabaçal is hair-raising;* motorists may prefer Alternative walk 1 below. Otherwise, either hire a taxi for a full day or pick one up at the Recta das Canhas (see Walk 35, page 122).

Short walks

1 **Rabaçal — Risco — Rabaçal.** 1.7km/1mi; 30min. Easy. Access as above. Follow the main walk for 13min and return the same way.

2 **Rabaçal — 25 Fontes — Rabaçal.** 5km/3mi; 1h40min. Easy. Access as above. (*Note:* This route used to be very vertiginous, but wooden fencing has been built. If the fencing falls into disrepair, those prone to vertigo may have to turn back.) Follow the main walk for 5min, then turn left down the path to the Levada das 25 Fontes. Do the main walk from the 21min-point to 25 Fontes and return the same way.

Alternative walks

1 **Rabaçal tunnel — Rabaçal levadas — Rabaçal tunnel.** 16km/10mi; 5h15min. Grade and equipment as main walk; take a torch as well. Access by 🚗. Because the road to Rabaçal is so narrow and vertiginous, you may prefer this approach. From the ER110 drive south on the ER211 and park about 2km downhill, by a derelict garage (now just a wall; 'Garagem' on the map). From there follow the dirt track on the opposite side of the road to the Rabaçal tunnel (**P**37c; 10min) and go through it (20min). You emerge at a sun-trap on the Levada das 25 Fontes (**P**37b). Follow the levada for a minute, then turn right up steps to the Risco levada and Rabaçal. Do the main walk, but don't climb back up to Rabaçal; return to the sun-trap and go through the tunnel, back to your car.

2 **Rabaçal levadas — Rocha Vermelha tunnel — Loreto.** 20.5km/ 12.7mi; about 6h. Grade: moderate, but you must be sure-footed and have a head for heights (**danger of vertigo** just before the tunnel). Equipment as main walk, plus torch. Access by taxi (see Walk 35, page 122); return on 🚌 80, 107, 115 or 142 from Loreto. Follow the main walk to the 3h05min-point; then, instead of climbing up to Rabaçal, continue through the Rocha Vermelha tunnel (20min), coming out in the Calheta Valley. Follow the levada to its tiny reservoir, then pick up Walk 35 to continue to Loreto (see page 124, just after the 2h50min-point).

Rabaçal is an enchanted fairyland of singing waterfalls, a favourite excursion spot for the islanders. Here at the head of Madeira's greatest valley, the Rabaçal house (**P**37a) lies dwarfed beneath emerald mountains. Three levadas converge here; each has its own 'personality', and this walk lets you make friends with all three.

The walk begins just where the tarred road ends at **Rabaçal**. Turn right down the dirt track. In **3min** you find yourself on the highest levada (1030m/3380ft), the **Levada do Risco**. Pass a fork to the Levada das 25 Fontes in **5min** and in **9min** ford a spillway created by a waterfall on the

Mossy trail beside the Levada do Risco. Notice how some of the heath trees grow out horizontally across the levada.

right. Around here the levada is flanked by an exceedingly beautiful mossy 'carpet' (see above), and the banks are built up high to cope with a great flow. At a fork, keep right on concrete to a viewpoint (**13min**; *P*37d), where the **Risco** waterfall cascades into a pool from a height of 100m/325ft. A tunnel on the right disgorges even more water, drawn from below the Urze peak. From here you can see the levada continue around the head of the gorge and along the valley opposite to its source in the Ribeira Grande, but this dangerous route is closed to walkers. Look below, across the valley, to see a second channel cut into the mountainside: this is the 'middle' levada, leading to 25 Fontes ('25 Springs'). If you don't mind getting soaked, you can venture under the falls to see Risco's pool, but beyond there the levada is unsafe.

Now retrace your steps to the fork to 25 Fontes (**21min**). Turn right and descend stone steps to reach the **Levada das 25 Fontes** (altitude 960m/3150ft). Turn right and you will see the Risco waterfall again, from a lower level: in **40min** you come to the head of the gorge where they dive down. Then cross the bed of the **Ribeira Grande**, to meet a tiny waterhouse: water is usually gushing out of its front door… From here on the levada channel is only 30cm/1ft wide in places, and there are drops at the left of up to 30m/100ft. But even without fencing we never found this levada vertiginous because, unlike most others, it is built up off the path, not sunk into it. The concrete edge of the levada is at waist level, and you can hold on to it for moral support if the drops worry you. It's cooling to run your hands in the water on a hot day.

In **1h** you pass the path down left to the Levada da Rocha Vermelha; ignore it for now. In about **1h10min**, in a tributary of the Cedros River, you reach a path leading up right (by a sluice), and at once you see the **25 Fontes** — a semi-circular bowl into which tumble down many sparkling waterfalls (but, alas, no longer 25). It's a lovely place to paddle under ferns (**P**37e).

From here return to the path passed 10 minutes earlier. Turn down right (perhaps passing some beehives on your right). Keep to the main zigzag path to prevent erosion. Soon you can see the levada below. The **Levada da Rocha Vermelha** (**1h35min**), at 850m/2790ft, is the lowest of the Rabaçal levadas. A keepers' house sits below on your right. This levada is much wider than the other two and is the newest of the three. Turn right on it, back up into the valley of the **Ribeira dos Cedros**. There are waterfalls left, right and centre! You cross the Cedros ravine on the levada channel (covered with concrete slabs), and find a tunnel on your right: water is flowing in from mountains on the east side of the Seixal River, some 4km/2.5mi away. Turn left on the levada and follow it round the valley. Soon you're just opposite the *levadeiros'* house; some 215m/700ft directly above it you see the Rabaçal houses. Notice how the levada narrows beyond each tributary, as you head towards its source. In **2h10min** you might like to take a break at a grassy promontory, from where there is a magnificent view of the Ribeira da Janela 200m/650ft below.

Time constraints will limit the distance you can walk on this levada; we stop after **2h25min**, where the thick blue line ends on the map*. From here return the same way, enjoying grassy verges and the aroma of wild mint, open views and shady heath-tree bowers (cover photograph). You'll be back at the keepers' cottage in **2h55min**. Stay on the levada, passing the path where you came down to it, and turning up into the **Ribeira Grande**. The Risco falls and the 25 Fontes Levada are visible ahead and above you. Across this wild gully yawns the Rocha Vermelha tunnel (Alternative walk 2); it disgorges in the Calheta Valley near the path of Walk 35.

A bridge crosses the river, to the tunnel, but carry on past it, to the sluices and rock pools (**3h05min**), where you can take a break below the roaring (Risco) falls. Then walk back, cross the bridge, and turn *sharp left* up a stone-laid path (masked by ferns at first), to begin the climb of 185m/600ft back to Rabaçal. In 15 minutes you reach the **Levada das 25 Fontes**, where you turn right. Ten minutes later, just before a high tunnel (Walk 35), steps on the left take you up to the picnic area at **Rabaçal** (**3h45min**).

*About 15 minutes further on, you would find steps similar to those in the photograph on page 127 — but over 300 of them! *Experts* might like to climb them (the descent is horrendously vertiginous) and pursue the levada to its source (another 50min; *not* shown on the map).

38 LEVADA DA RIBEIRA GRANDE

See map on pages 124-125　　　　**Distance:** 6km/3.7mi; 1h50min

Grade: easy, but some of the clay paths are very slippery; you must be sure-footed and have a head for heights (slight **possibility of vertigo**).

Equipment: stout shoes, picnic, water

How to get there and return: 🚗 car to the parking area on the ER110, at the top of the road to Rabaçal (Car tours 5, 6)

H ere's a short ramble that is easily combined with a day's touring on the Paúl da Serra. Since this levada is not named on any maps, we have tried to christen it appropriately: it takes its source in the Ribeira Grande, almost 300m/1000ft above the levadas followed in Walk 37. At 1300m/4265ft, this is the 'penthouse suite' of the Ribeira Grande levadas. But unlike the levadas in Walk 37, this one is twinned with the Levada do Paúl (Walk 35) and flows into the reservoir on the ER110.

Start out at the car park: walk down the Rabaçal road for 120m/yds, then fork right on a path. This takes you to the wide **Levada da Ribeira Grande**. A pretty amble brings you quickly to a small semi-circular reservoir, which may be brimming with tiny trout (**12min**; *P*38). Immediately past it, you cross the **Ribeira do Alecrím** (Rosemary River).

After a narrow, unprotected stretch with a sheer drop to the left (amply wide and quickly passed), you come to 20 steps (similar to those in the photograph on page 127). These take you up to a fine viewpoint over the Ribeira da Janela and your starting point (**30min**) and then into the valley of the **Ribeira Grande**, from where you will have glimpses down over the three levadas followed in Walk 37.

When you reach the source of the levada in the wide river bed (**55min**), a waterfall, rock pools and bird song beckon you to bide a while. Then return the same way to the CAR PARK on the ER110 (**1h50min**).

Rock pools and waterfall in the bed of the Ribeira Grande

39 PICO RUIVO DO PAÚL

See map pages 124-125; see also photograph page 34

Distance: 4km/2.5mi; 1h15min

Grade: easy climb/descent of 150m/ 500ft, but avoid the climb to the summit if there is any sign of mist descending; follow the levada to find your way back to your car.

Equipment: stout shoes, sunhat, picnic, water

How to get there and return: 🚗 car to the junction of the ER110 to Bica da Cana and the ER208 to Estanquinhos, by a narrow levada (Car tours 5, 6)

By now it won't be a secret to you that the Paúl da Serra is one of our favourite places on Madeira — and with the new motorway you're there in a trice. Wonderful for picnicking and doing a few short walks on a 'lazy day'. This is another stunner!

Start out at the road JUNCTION: head north in the setting shown on page 34, following the grassy banks beside the narrow blue ribbon of levada. The levada squiggles its way through woods (**10min**) and eventually crosses a track at a beautiful picnic setting (**P**39). Just three minutes later, beyond the water collection pit shown below, you reach the source of the levada (**20min**). From here just follow the trampled bracken up to the top of **Pico Ruivo do Paúl** (**30min** — or even **45min** on a hot day). From here there is a wonderful view east, similar to the view in the photograph on page 119.

Rather than return the same way, head south down the hill and make your way (no path) over the moorland, back to your car at the JUNCTION (**1h15min**).

View towards the Janela Valley from the water pit

40 FROM PRAZERES TO PAÚL DO MAR

Map pages 134-135, photo page 15   **Distance:** 5km/3mi; 1h35min

Grade: strenuous descent of about 650m/2100ft *in full sun*; you must be sure-footed and have a head for heights (**danger of vertigo**). *Avoid in damp weather, when the path would be slippery and treacherous.*

Note: To do the walk in reverse (easier on the knees and less vertiginous), walk through a narrow gap between houses, a few metres/yards uphill from the bar on the quay in Paúl do Mar, *before* the road bends left.

Equipment: stout shoes (walking boots preferable), sunhat, whistle, walking stick, picnic, water; extra cardigan and anorak in cool weather

How to get there: 🚌 80, 107, 142 or 🚗 to Prazeres; by car, park at the Hotel Jardim Atlántico (Car tour 6)
To return: 🚗 taxi from Paúl do Mar back to your car, or to the ER101 in time for a return bus. Book a taxi at the office/bar by the church in Prazeres (there *are* taxis at Paúl do Mar, but they are sometimes away on day trips to Funchal). Alternatively, climb back up to Prazeres (exhausting on a hot day), *if you are sure you can catch your return bus!*

Having tweezered a few dozen cactus spines out of our arms and legs, here is the only zigzag descent in the southwest that we can heartily recommend. (The cactus spines were acquired on *other* forays, none of which we would recommend to 'Landscapers'.) But this is *the* 5-star route in the area, a wonderfully exhilarating descent that spirals you down to photogenic Paúl do Mar. The focal points are the ochre-to-burgundy volcanic cliffs, a Swiss cheese landscape of caves and rivulets plastered with houseleeks and Pride of Madeira. Take plenty of film!

Begin on the ER222 at **Prazeres**. Follow the signposted road through bucolic countryside to the HOTEL JARDIM ATLÁNTICO (**30min**). At the far end of the hotel car park, walk south downhill on a concrete pavement with lamp-posts (signposted 'VEREDA DO PAÚL'). Already there are wonderful views over Jardim do Mar to the left and Paúl do Mar below. Soon steps take you down to an exquisite old cobbled trail. Some 10 minutes down, someone has thoughtfully placed a bench below pines, where you can sit and contemplate the fields and terraces below Maloeira on the plateau and Raposeira on the ridge beyond it (*P*40).

Soon the path goes into a roller-coaster descent and, just when you think you cannot stomach the pitch any longer, you're saved from the abyss by a zig or a zag. As you near the sea, look back into the great cleft where the Seca and Cova rivers come together and plummet 400m/1300ft in a graceful waterfall. After crossing a stone bridge over the **Ribeira Seca** in a delightful setting, descend for another five minutes, then turn down left to the tiny quay at **Paúl do Mar** (**1h35min**), where the falls crash onto the pebbly shore just behind the colourful fishing boats.

If you haven't arranged for someone to collect you, walk on to the restaurant, where they can call a taxi.

41 LEVADA CALHETA–PONTA DO PARGO

See also map on page 124 and touring map

Grade: easy   **Distance:** as individual walk suggestions

Equipment: stout shoes, sunhat, picnic, water

How to get there: 🚐 107 or 142 or 🚕 to Raposeira

To return: 🚐 80, 107 or 142 back to your base or your car

The Levada Calheta–Ponta do Pargo (see notes on page 123) is just perfect for strolling. As it contours along the sun-drenched plains above the coast, it gives you superb views up to the Paúl da Serra, where scudding clouds create an ever-changing mosaic on the hillsides. Gorgeous all year round, these walks are perhaps at their best in high summer, when the levada is full to brimming, and the agapanthus and hydrangeas are in bloom. You stroll under pine and eucalyptus, by ferny glens and banks of lilies. While there is ample shade, much of the route is exposed; adequate sun protection is *essential*.

Left: the Levada Calheta–Ponta do Pargo in July; right: you'll be a source of some curiosity to the locals!

Walk suggestions: Both of our suggestions begin below (just south of) Raposeira church, but you can join the **Levada Calheta–Ponta do Pargo** at other convenient points. The touring map shows you at a glance where the levada crosses the road. If you are driving, there are several places to park along the quiet ER101, for example 2km west of Raposeira church, at the turn-off down to Fajã da Ovelha. Perhaps combine your levada walk with a visit to the fine viewpoint over Paúl do Mar at Raposeira (2km return), or just amble down one of the grassy trails overlooking the lighthouse at Ponta do Pargo.

1   Follow the levada east from Raposeira. You can leave it for the ER222 at Prazeres (4.7km/3mi; 1h15min), Lombo dos Moinhos (9km/5.6mi; 2h15min), or the power station above Calheta (20.5km/12.7mi; 5h). Beyond the power station you could join Walk 35 and continue to Loreto (26.5km/16.5mi; 6h30min; map pages 124-125, notes page 125).

2   Head west from Raposeira (see below and touring map). You cross the road at Lombada dos Marinheiros (9km/5.6mi; 2h15min), but must descend to Ponta do Pargo (15km/9.3mi; 3h45min). The levada ends at Ribeira da Vaca, served only by 🚐 80 (21.5km/13.3mi; 5h20min).

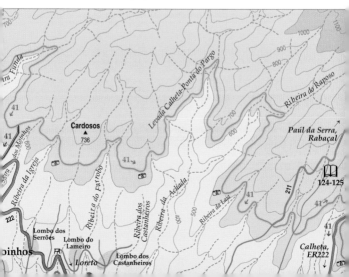

42 LEVADA DA CENTRAL DA RIBEIRA DA JANELA

Distance: up to 9km/5.6mi; 2h30min

Grade: easy, but you must be sure-footed and have a head for heights; **possibility of vertigo**.

Equipment: stout shoes (walking boots preferable), long trousers, cardigans, anorak, sunhat, rainhat, picnic, water, whistle, *optional torch*

How to get there and return: 🚗 car or taxi to the reservoir above Porto Moniz. Ask a taxi driver for 'Levada da Central, Lamaceiros' ('Lah-mah-**say**-roosh'). By car, drive uphill out of Porto Moniz: 3.5km up from the roundabout with a statue by the petrol station, turn left for Lamaceiros (signposted). Keep straight at any forks. Go through Lamaceiros (keeping to the left of the church, 4.5km from the roundabout). When the road bends right (4.8km), go straight ahead for 100-200m and park either side of the levada (its reservoir is to the left). Or 🚌 139 to Porto Moniz, then taxi as above. Walk 1.3km back to the ER101 at the Lamaceiros turn-off for the return bus (80 or 150). Also: 🚌 150 from São Vicente to/from the Lamaceiros turn-off (add 1.3km each way); bus timings allow 3h for the walk.

Short walk: to the second filtration point and back. 3.5km/2.2mi; 1h. Easy. Follow the main walk for 30min and return the same way.

From the western flanks of the great Janela Valley you look across to the stupendous array of tiny terraces tumbling helter-skelter from Ribeira da Janela down to the river far below. Then you leave the cultivation behind, for ferny glens,

In about 30 minutes the levada widens by a second filtration point. The path is lined with fruit trees intertwined with passion flowers. This is an especially beautiful picnic spot (a second setting for Picnic 42). Further along you'll walk beneath beech trees and indigenous laurels and skirt high escarpments bearded with a great variety of ferns.

mossy cliffs and prime-val woodlands.

Start out at the RESERVOIR and follow the wide levada (inaugurated 1965) past a picnic table (**3min**; *P*42) and a then a wide filtration point. Huge bushes of fennel, apple and fig trees, and garlands of passion flowers herald the next filtration tank (**30min**; *P*42). Five minutes later, notice the cables and pulleys used for moving supplies between the watercourse and the valley floor. Down by the river one of the most impressive expanses of terracing on the island stretches out below you.

Within **45min** the sure of foot will reach a ferny glen in the upper reaches of the **Ribeira da Cova Negra**. Soon you skirt a rock wall pouring with rainwater. In **1h** you are looking straight up the Janela Valley; if you have binoculars, you will easily see the Rabaçal houses from here (Walks 35 and 37).

The walk ends in **1h15min**, when you meet a tunnel* in the **Ribeira da Quebrada**. Turn back here, to catch the bus or return to your car near the RESERVOIR (**2h30min**).

*It takes 10 minutes to get through this tunnel, but there are seven more behind it, one of which takes about 30 minutes. *Experts* could follow the *extremely vertiginous* levada to the keepers' house and then the source (about 2h30min from here; strong torch and raingear needed ... but you will get soaked anyway). From the keepers' house a steep path, then a track climbs 850m/2800ft (7km/4.3mi; about 3h) to Fonte do Bispo. This route is *not* shown on any of our maps. Arrange to be met on the ER110 at the 'Galhano' signpost, opposite Fonte do Bispo (Car tours 5 and 6).

137

BUS TIMETABLES

Below is a list of destinations covered by these timetables. Numbers following place names are *bus numbers;* they are arranged below in numerical order. *But note that all orange 'town' buses are on page 142.* See page 9 for more bus information and pages 10-11 for bus departure points. **No buses run on Christmas day.**

Achadinha 111
Águas Mansas 60, 77, 110
Assomada 2, 20, 23, 25, 53, 78, 113
Babosas *town* 🚐 22
Barreira *shuttle* 🚐 91
Boa Morte 127, 148
Boaventura 6, 103, 132
Boqueirão 60, 110
Cabo Girão 154
Camacha 29, 77
Campanário 4, 6, 7, 80, 107, 115, 123, 139, 142, 148
Canhas 80, 107, 115, 142
Caniçal 113
Caniço 2, 110, 113, 114, 155
Corticeiras 96
Cruz 53, 78
Cruzinhas 103, 138
Curral das Freiras 81
Eira do Serrado (turn-off) 81
Encumeada 6, 139
Estreito de C.d. Lobos 3, 4, 6, 7, 80, 96, 107, 115, 123, 139, 142, 148, 154

Faial 53, 78, 103, 138
Fontes 127, 148
Formiga 4, 80, 107, 115, 142
Ilha de São Jorge 103, 132, 138
Jardim Botânico *town* 🚐 29, 30, 31
Lombada *town* 🚐 1, 3
Lombo Grande 60
Loreto 80, 107, 115, 142
Machico 20, 23, 53, 78, 113, 156
Madalena do Mar 4
Maroços 156
Monte 103, 138, *town* 🚐 20, 21
Nogueira 110, 114
Palheiro Ferreiro 29, 77, *town* 🚐 36, 37, 47
Paúl do Mar 142
Pico do Facho (turn-off to) 113
Pinheiro das Voltas *town* 🚐 16A
Poiso 103, 138

Ponta do Pargo 80, 107, 150
Ponta do Sol 4 (direct) or 80, 107, 115, 142 (turn-off on the ER222)
Portela 20, 53, 78
Porto da Cruz 53, 78
Porto Moniz 80, 139, 150
Prazeres 80, 107, 115, 142
Raposeira 80, 107, 142
Ribeira Brava 4, 6, 7, 80, 107, 115, 127, 139, 142
Ribeira Seca 113
Ribeirinha 111
Ribeiro Frio 103, 138
Romeiros *town* 🚐 29
Santa 107, 150
Santana 103, 132, 138
Santo da Serra 20, 25, 77, 78
São João Latrão *town* 🚐 47
São Jorge 103, 132, 138
São Vicente 6, 132, 139, 150
Sítio Quatro Estradas 77
Stadium *town* 🚐 45
Trapiche *town* 🚐 10A, 11; *shuttle* 🚐 91

2 Funchal • Assomada (journey time 35min)
Departs Funchal: 07.30, 08.20#, 08.30▫, 09.15#, 10.00, 11.00, 11.45•, 12.00•, 13.00, 14.00*, 15.00, 16.00, 16.30•, 17.00*, 17.45*, 18.00•, 18.45*, 19.00•, 19.30*, 20.15*, 20.30•, 21.00*, 22.30, 23.45

Departs Assomada: 06.45+, 07.00*, 07.30*, 08.10*, 08.30•, 09.10+, 09.30▫•, 10.00+, 11.00, 11.40*, 12.00•, 12.25*, 13.30•, 13.45*, 14.40*, 14.45•, 15.45*, 16.45*, 17.00•, 17.45, 18.30*, 19.00•, 19.30*, 21.10+, 21.30▫•, 21.45+, 23.10

3 Funchal • Estreito de Câmara de Lobos (journey time 45min)
Departs Funchal: 10.30+, 12.00+, 12.45+, 14.05•, 14.45▫, 15.05+, 16.00+, 16.40+, 17.00•, 17.35▫, 18.00▫, 18.05¶, 18.15+, 18.45▫, 19.15+

Departs Estreito: 07.00•, 07.15+, 08.00+, 08.15*, 11.30+, 13.05+, 14.00+, 15.05▫•, 15.40▫, 17.00+

4 Funchal • Madalena do Mar (via Ribeira Brava and Ponta do Sol)

Funchal	10.00*	12.00+	14.00*	17.30‡	Madalena	11.45•	12.50*	
Ribeira Brava	11.25*	13.25+	15.15*	19.00‡	Ponta do Sol	11.55•	13.00*	
Formiga	11.50*	13.50+	15.45*	19.15‡	Formiga	12.05•	13.10*	
Ponta do Sol	12.00*	14.00+	15.55*	19.20‡	Ribeira Brava	12.20•	13.30*	
Madalena	12.10*	00.00	00.00	19.30‡	Funchal	13.25•	14.50*	

6 Funchal • Boaventura (via Ribeira Brava and São Vicente)

Funchal	07.35	13.35*	17.30	Boaventura	06.00*	07.15	15.00
Estreito C.d.L.	08.10	14.10*	18.10	P. Delgada	06.20*	07.30	15.20
Campanário	08.35	14.30*	18.30	S. Vicente	06.35*	07.55	15.30
Ribeira Brava	08.50	14.40*	18.45	Encumeada	07.05*	08.25	15.55
Encumeada	09.30	15.20*	19.25	Ribeira Brava	07.35*	08.50	16.30
São Vicente	10.10	15.45*	19.50	Campanário	07.50*	09.05	16.45
P. Delgada	10.30	16.25*	20.20	Estreito C.d.L.	08.10*	09.45	17.20
Boaventura	11.00	16.50*	20.45	Funchal	08.50*	10.25	17.50

+Mon-Fri only; *not Sundays or holidays; ‡only Mon/Wed/Fri; •only Sundays/holidays; #not Saturdays; ▫only Saturdays; ¶in the school season only

7 Funchal • Ribeira Brava (journey time 1h30min)

Departs Funchal: 06.45*, 07.55+ (via the Via Rápida), 09.30+, 10.05•, 10.50*, 12.05+, 13.30□•,
15.30, 17.00, 18.00+ (via the Via Rápida), 18.30■, 20.15, 22.30+, 23.30

Departs Ribeira Brava: 06.05, 08.15*, 09.00+ (via the Via Rápida), 11.00*, 11.45•, 12.30□, 12.35+,
13.35•, 15.30□•, 17.15, 18.35, 19.00+ (via the Via Rápida), 22.10

20 Funchal • Machico • Santo da Serra (via Portela)

Funchal	07.15*	09.30+	12.40	16.30+	19.15+	20.45+
Machico	08.05*	10.20+	13.30	17.20+	20.05+	21.35+
Santo da Serra *(arrives)*	08.45*	11.00+	14.10	18.00+	20.45+	22.15+
Santo da Serra *(departs)*	06.30*	08.00*	09.45*	10.00••	12.20+	14.45+	16.15••
Machico	07.10*	08.40*	10.25*	10.40••	13.00+	15.25+	16.55••
Funchal	08.00*	09.30*	11.15*	00.00	13.50+	16.20+	17.45••

Passes Portela about 10min before arriving/after departing Santo da Serra

23 Funchal • Machico (journey time 45min direct express, 55min via Gaula)

Departs Funchal: 17.15+ *express*, 18.15+ *express*, 21.30* (via Gaula)

Departs Machico: 07.00+ *express*, 07.30* (via Gaula), 07.45+ *express*, 09.30* (via Gaula),
18.30• (via Gaula), 22.45*

25 Funchal • Santo da Serra (via Santa Cruz; journey time 1h10min)

Departs Funchal: 08.45••

29 Funchal • Camacha (journey time 40min)

Departs Funchal: 08.00*, 09.00, 10.00, 11.00, 11.45*, 12.30•, 13.00+, 13.30, 14.30, 15.30, 16.30+,
17.00, 17.30*, 18.00#, 18.30*, 18.45+, 19.00, 19.30+, 20.00#, 20.30, 22.00, 22.30

Departs Camacha: 07.00, 07.05+, 07.15+, 07.45+, 08.15, 08.45*, 09.45, 10.45, 11.45, 12.30*,
13.15, 13.45+, 14.15, 15.15, 16.15, 17.45, 18.15*, 18.45#, 19.15*, 19.45, 21.00□•, 22.45

53 Funchal • Machico • Portela • Porto da Cruz • Faial

Funchal	00.00	10.00*	13.00+	13.15□	00.00	16.15+	18.10+	18.15•	19.15+
Machico	09.00+	10.50*	13.50+	14.05□	14.30••	17.05+	19.00+	19.05•	20.05+
Portela	09.25+	11.15*	14.15+	14.30□	15.00••	17.30+	19.30+	19.30•	20.30+
Porto da Cruz	09.35+	11.30*	14.30+	14.45□	15.15••	17.45+	19.50+	19.45•	20.45+
Faial *(arrives)*	09.45+	11.45*	14.45+	15.00□	15.30••	18.00+	00.00	20.00•	21.00+
Faial *(departs)*	05.45+	07.45+	10.00	13.00+	13.30••	15.30*	17.00*	18.15¶	*The*
Porto da Cruz	05.55+	07.55+	10.10	13.10+	13.40••	15.40*	17.10*	18.25¶	*18.15*
Portela	06.10+	08.10+	10.25	13.25+	13.55••	15.55*	17.25*	18.40¶	*bus*
Machico	06.35+	08.45+	10.55	13.50+	14.20••	16.30*	18.00*	19.00¶	*starts at*
Funchal	07.30+	00.00	11.55	00.00	00.00	17.30*	18.50*		*Cruz,*

east of Faial

60 Funchal • Boqueirão (via Gaula; journey time 1h)

Departs Funchal: 11.00, 13.30*, 17.00+, 18.25+, 19.15, 20.30+
Buses pass Gaula approx. 10min and Lombo Grande 5min before Boqueirão.

Departs Boqueirão: 06.15*, 06.30•, 06.45+, 07.30*, 08.30*, 12.00*, 17.00
Buses pass Lombo Grande approx. 5min and Gaula 10min after Boqueirão.

77 Funchal • Santo da Serra (via Camacha)

Funchal	07.35*	08.30•	10.30	14.00	16.30	18.00*	19.15#
Camacha	08.10*	09.10•	11.10	14.40	17.10	18.40*	19.55#
Sítio Quatro Estradas	08.40*	09.40•	11.40	15.10	17.40	19.10*	20.25#
Santo da Serra *(arrives)*	08.50*	09.50•	11.50	15.20	17.50	19.20*	20.35#
Santo da Serra *(departs)*	07.00	09.00*	10.00•	12.00#	16.15	18.00	20.30+
Sítio Quatro Estradas	07.05	09.05*	10.05•	12.05#	16.20	18.05	20.35+
Camacha	07.40	09.40*	10.40•	12.40#	16.55	18.40	21.10+
Funchal	08.20	10.20*	11.20•	13.20#	17.35	19.20	21.50+

+Mon-Fri; ■not on 31 Dec or 1 Jan; □only Saturdays; *not Sundays or holidays; ‡only Mon/Wed/
Fri; •only Sundays/holidays; ••only Sundays; †not Sundays or the first Saturday in Sept.; #not
Saturdays; §Sat/Sun/holidays only; ¶in the school season only; ÷except 1, 6 Jan, 25, 26 Dec,
via the coastal road and Ponta do Sol; **only on holidays; ▲Mondays to Saturdays, also holidays;
++Tue, Wed, Thur, Fri only

78 Funchal • Machico • Faial (via Santo da Serra, Portela, Porto da Cruz)

Funchal	08.00•	12.40**	16.30▫	Faial	06.45▲	17.30•
Machico	08.50•	13.30**	17.20▫	Machico	07.45▲	18.30•
Faial *(arrives)*	10.00•	14.40**	18.30▫	Funchal *(arrives)*	08.35▲	19.30•

From Machico add approx. 30min to Portela, 40min to Santo da Serra, 1h to Porto da Cruz. From Faial add approx. 10min to Porto da Cruz, 20min to Portela, 30min to Santo da Serra.

80 Porto Moniz • Funchal (via Prazeres)

Porto Moniz *(departs)* 16.00; Ponta do Pargo 16.50; Prazeres 17.15; Loreto 17.45; Formiga 18.15; Ribeira Brava 18.40; Funchal *(arrives)* 20.05
Departs Funchal for Porto Moniz Saturdays only (not holidays) at 14.35; arrives 19.00

81 Funchal • Curral das Freiras (via Eira do Serrado and Cumial; journey time 1h15min)

Departs Funchal: 06.50•, 07.45*, 08.45*, 09.15•, 10.30*, 11.30, 13.15*, 13.30•, 15.15+, 16.30, 18.30+, 19.30, 20.30+, 21.45, 23.45
Departs Curral (from Seara Velha terminus): 06.30*, 07.30+, 07.40•, 08.45*, 10.00*, 10.30•, 11.45+, 12.00▫, 12.30•, 13.15*, 14.30, 16.15+, 17.45, 19.30+, 20.30, 21.30+

96 Funchal • Corticeiras (via Estreito de Câmara de Lobos; journey time 1h)

Mondays to Fridays
Departs Funchal: 07.00, 07.30ᶠ, 08.05, 09.05ᶠ, 09.45, 10.45, 11.45, 12.15, 13.15, 14.15, 15.15, 16.15ᶠ, 16.45, 17.30, 17.30ᶠ, 18.00, 18.15, 18.15ᶠ, 18.30, 18.45, 19.15ᶠ, 19.50, 21.05
Departs Corticeiras: approximately half-hourly from 05.00 until 09.05, then 10.15, 11.00, 12.00, 12.55, 13.30ᶠ, 14.30, 15.30, 16.30, 17.30, 18.00, 19.00, 20.00

Saturdays, Sundays and holidays (only convenient times for walkers are shown here)
Departs Funchal: 07.00, 08.05, 09.15ᶠ, 11.15, 12.05▫, 13.05•, 13.05ᴰᶠ, 14.05▫, 15.05, 16.05
Departs Corticeiras: 12.30▫, 12.45•, 13.05▫, 14.05, 15.05▫, 16.05, 17.05, 17.30▫, 18.35, 20.00
Arrives Estreito 45min after departing Funchal and 15min after departing Corticeiras.

103 Funchal • Boaventura *(intermediate times are approximate — arrive early!)*

Funchal	07.15	13.30*	16.00*	18.00	Boaventura	05.30*	07.00	12.00*	16.00
Poiso	08.15	14.30*	17.00*	19.00	Vigia road	06.20*	07.50	12.50*	16.40
Rib. Frio	08.25	14.40*	17.10*	19.10	São Jorge	06.30*	08.00	13.00*	16.50
Cruzinhas	08.45	15.00*	17.30*	19.30	Ilha	06.40*	08.10	13.10*	17.00
Faial	09.00	15.15*	17.45*	19.45	Santana	07.00*	08.30	13.30*	17.30
Santana	09.30	15.45*	18.15*	20.15	Faial	07.30*	09.00	14.00*	18.00
Ilha	09.50	16.05*	18.35*	20.35	Cruzinhas	07.45*	09.15	14.15*	18.15
São Jorge	10.00	16.15*	18.45*	20.45	Rib. Frio	08.05*	09.35	14.35*	18.35
Vigia road	10.10	16.25*	18.55*	20.55	Poiso	08.15*	19.45	14.45*	18.45
Boaventura	11.00	17.15*	19.45*	21.45	Funchal	09.00*	10.45	15.45*	19.45

107 Funchal • Ponta do Pargo (and sometimes Santa; see note)

Funchal	08.05	15.05		Ponta do Pargo	05.00++	00.00	14.35
Ribeira Brava	09.20	16.20		Prazeres	05.35++	06.30+	15.05
Formiga	10.00	00.00		Canhas	06.25++	07.25+	15.55
Canhas	10.15	17.00		Formiga	06.35++	00.00	16.05
Prazeres	11.30	18.00		Ribeira Brava	06.55++	08.00+	16.40
Ponta do Pargo	12.00	18.45		Funchal	07.35++	09.25+	17.50

From Mon-Sat the 15.05 bus goes on 45min to Santa; the 05.00 bus begins 30min earlier at Santa

110 Funchal • Boqueirão (via Caniço and Nogueira; journey time 40min)

Departs Funchal: 07.45•, 09.15+, 09.45+, 12.30*, 15.30+, 16.00▫, 16.15+, 18.30#
Departs Boqueirão: 07.30*, 08.45#, 10.00+, 10.30+, 13.45*, 17.00+

111 Funchal • Achadinha (via Ribeirinha; journey time 1h)

Departs Funchal: 07.30+, 08.30+, 10.15+, 13.00, 15.45+, 18.15+, 19.05+, 19.45+
Departs Achadinha: 06.45+, 07.15+, 07.45+, 09.15+, 11.00+, 12.15+, 13.45, 16.30+

113 Funchal • Machico (journey time 50min) • Caniçal (journey time 25min; see note)

Departs Funchal (for Machico): 07.30, 08.30*, 09.00ᴾ, 11.15*ᴾ, 12.15*, 12.15•ᴾ, 13.30•, 13.45+, 14.30*ᴾ, 15.00#, 15.00•ᴾ, 15.30*, 15.45•, 16.30•, 17.15*, 18.10+, 18.15*, 19.00•, 19.30+, 19.45▫, 20.00+, 21.00•, 22.30; *Departs Machico (for Caniçal):* 07.15*, 07.45+, 08.20, 09.20, 09.50, 11.00¶, 12.05, 13.05, 15.20, 15.50, 16.20, 17.20, 18.05, 19.05, 19.50, 20.20, 20.35, 23.20

Departs Caniçal (for Machico): 05.45*, 06.45, 07.30*, 08.30+, 09.30, 10.30, 11.45*ᴾ, 13.10*ᴾ, 14.10, 14.10•ᴾ, 17.10ᴾ, 18.10*, 19.10•, 19.45*, 21.00•▫; *Departs Machico (for Funchal):* 06.00, 06.30, 07.00, 07.45, 08.30, 08.45, 09.45, 10.45, 11.45, 12.00, 13.15, 13.25, 14.15, 14.25, 17.15, 17.25, 18.25, 19.25, 20.00, 21.15, 22.45

ᴾ*goes on to Prainha and returns from Prainha five minutes earlier. In summer only (June to September), the buses that go to Prainha now go all the way to/return from Abra Bay.* **See other symbol codes opposite.**

114 Funchal • Nogueira (via Caniço; journey time approximately 45min)
Departs Funchal: 06.30*, 07.35, 08.45□•, 09.30+, 10.00□•, 11.15, 13.45*, 14.30, 16.30, 17.15+, 17.40, 18.50, 19.20*, 20.30, 22.00, 22.45+, 23.30, 00.15+
Departs Nogueira: 06.00, 07.00, 07.30+, 08.00+, 08.15, 09.25□•, 10.15+, 10.40□•, 11.55, 14.30*, 15.15, 17.15, 18.00+, 18.20, 19.30, 21.15, 22.15+, 22.45, 23.30+

115 Funchal • Estreito da Calheta (journey time 2h40min)
Departs Funchal 15.00+; then: Ribeira Brava 16.15+, Formiga 16.45+, Canhas 17.00+, Estreito da Calheta 17.40+; *goes on to Prazeres* (add 10min)
Departs Estreito: 11.45+; then: Canhas 12.30+, Ribeira Brava 13.15, Funchal 14.25
Bus departing Estreito 11.45 follows the coast road and does not call at Formiga.

123 Funchal • Campanário (journey time 1h05min)
Departs Funchal: 11.30+, 13.00+, 18.05□, 19.00□; *Departs Campanário:* 14.30+

127 Ribeira Brava • Boa Morte (journey time 20min) • Fontes (journey time 30min)
Departs Ribeira Brava: 08.15+★, 11.10+★, 13.10+★   *Departs Fontes:* 08.45, 13.45
The 11.10 bus goes only to Boa Morte; returns from Boa Morte at 11.35.

132 Santana • São Vicente (*not on holidays;* journey time approximately 2h)
Departs Santana: 06.00*, 08.45•, 11.25 (only from Boaventura), 13.55¶ (only from Boaventura)
Departs São Vicente: 10.30+, 13.00+¶, 15.00, 17.00*

138 Funchal • Cabanas, São Jorge (via Ribeiro Frio; journey time 2h45min)
Departs Funchal: 11.30+, 16.30•, 19.00+; *Departs Cabanas:* 05.00+, 10.00#
For times to intermediate destinations such as Ribeiro Frio compare bus 103.

139 Funchal • Porto Moniz (journey time 3h15min)
Departs Funchal 09.00; then: Ribeira Brava 10.15, São Vicente 11.30; arrives Porto Moniz 12.05. *For returns to Funchal, see bus 80.*

142 Funchal • Ponta do Pargo (journey time 3h45min)
Departs Funchal: 16.00•, 17.35*; *Departs Ponta do Pargo:* 07.45+
For times to intermediate destinations such as Prazeres compare bus 107. At 17.35 three buses depart, one of which takes the coastal road via Calheta and terminates at Paúl do Mar.

148 Funchal • Boa Morte (journey time 1h25min)
Departs Funchal: 13.05*, 18.10*; *Departs Boa Morte:* 14.30*
On Mon, Wed, Fri the bus departing at 18.10 goes on to Fontes.

150 São Vicente • Santa (journey time 45min) • Ponta do Pargo (journey time 1h30min)
Departs São Vicente: 10.30, 16.30*, 20.00•; *Departs Ponta do Pargo:* 13.15
Buses call at Porto Moniz 25min after leaving São Vicente. The 10.30 bus goes on to Ponta do Pargo (arrives 12.00).

154 Funchal • Cabo Girão; journey time 1h)
Departs Funchal: 09.00+, 10.35□, 11.45+, 17.00+, 19.00+; *Departs Cabo Girão:* 10.30+, 11.50□•, 18.00+

155 Funchal • Ponta da Oliveira (via Garajau or **Figueirinhas; journey time 35min)
Mondays to Saturdays
Departs Funchal: 06.30, 07.35, 08.10, 09.30, 10.15, 11.30#, 12.30, 13.30, 14.15, 15.30, 16.30#, 17.15, 18.00, 19.15, 20.00#, 21.45#, 23.30#
Departs Ponta da Oliveira: 07.00, 08.10, 08.55, 10.10, 11.00, 12.10#, 13.10, 14.15, 15.00, 16.15, 17.10#, 18.00, 19.15, 20.00#, 22.45#

Sundays and holidays
Departs Funchal: 08.15, 09.30, 10.15, 13.30, 15.30, 17.15
Departs Ponta da Oliveira: 07.15, 09.00, 10.10, 11.00, 14.15, 16.15, 18.15

156 Funchal • Machico (journey time 50min) • Maroços (journey time 15min)
Departs Funchal: 06.45*, 08.00*, 10.30, 11.45, 13.15+, 13.45□, 16.00*, 17.30+, 17.45, 19.00*, 20.00▲, 20.30□, 21.30•, 23.45
Departs Maroços: 05.45, 06.15#, 06.45*, 07.30*, 08.15#, 09.45+, 11.30, 12.30*, 13.00•, 13.10□, 13.40+, 15.30*, 15.45•, 18.10+, 19.00+, 20.00•, 22.30•
Departs Machico 50min after departing Funchal and 15min after departing Maroços.

□only Saturdays; *not Sundays or holidays; •only Sundays/holidays; ★not Good Friday, 25, 26, 31 Dec, 1 Jan; #not Saturdays; +Mon-Fri only; □via Foro (takes the lower road to Jardim da Serra; you have to climb up to Corticeiras); **only on holidays; ▲Mondays to Saturdays, also holidays; ++Tue, Wed, Thur, Fri only; ¶in the school season only

HORARIOS DO FUNCHAL (orange town buses)

A helpful plan for tourists, showing all town bus routes and fare zones (but not departure times) is available from information kiosks on the Avenida do Mar; see ⓘ symbol on the town plan on pages 10-11. This plan also includes all routes of buses operated by Autocarros da Camacha *with* departure times. Timetables for individual routes of town buses should be available free from the information kiosk just east of the power station (no 33 on the plan). Weekly tourist passes are available at the same kiosk. Or buy a 'double ticket' (*bilhete duplo;* also available in carnets of five tickets); these give you two bus journeys (not necessarily return trips) for little more than the cost of one. Otherwise, pay the driver as you board (keep small notes and coins handy). It is not possible to list all departure times in the limited space below; where specific services *are* shown, only the departure times you are most likely to use are listed. Note also that these departure times change frequently; re-check departure times at the bus shelters shown on the town plan.

1 Lombada ('Ponta da Laranjeira' bus; journey time approx. 30min) ■

2 Quebradas ('Papagaio Verde' bus; journey time approx. 30min) ■

3 Lombada (journey time approx 30min) ■

4 Amparo (journey time approx. 20min)
Services too numerous to list; generally every 20 minutes (hourly on weekends).

6 Lido (journey time approx. 20min) ■
Restricted Sunday service, except in summer. Check at the bus stop!

11 Trapiche (journey time approx. 30min)
Services too numerous to list; generally half-hourly (hourly on weekends), but there is a two-hour gap in both directions between 14.00 and 16.00.
A 10A 'Chamorra' bus also serves Trapiche with equal frequency (including a service at around 15.00 on weekends), but be sure to ask the driver if the bus is going to Trapiche!

16A Pinheiro das Voltas (journey time approx. 30min)
Departs Funchal: 08.00+, 08.50•, 09.15•, 09.50, 11.05, 12.05, 13.05, 14.00, 14.55+, 16.05+, 16.30•, 16.50+, 17.05*
Departs Pinheiro das Voltas: 10.40*, 11.40, 12.40, 13.35, 14.30, 15.40+, 16.40+, 17.05•, 17.30+, 17.40*, 18.05•, 18.25+, 18.40*, 19.05•, 19.40*, 19.55•, 20.40+

20, 21 Monte (journey time approx. 30min) ■ see also bus 22
You can walk between Monte and Babosas in 10 minutes, past the Monte Palace Gardens.

22 Babosas (journey time approx. 30min) ■ see also buses 20, 21
Services too numerous to list; generally hourly every day of the week. In 'rush hours' service is half-hourly.
You can walk between Monte and Babosas in 10 minutes, past the Monte Palace Gardens.

29 Romeiros (via the Jardim Botânico; journey time approx. 30min)
Departs Funchal: 07.00*, 07.20*, 07.45, 08.20*, 08.50, 09.55•, 10.30*, 11.00, 12.05+, 12.35, 13.05, 13.30, 15.30, 17.35, 18.00+, 18.35, 19.00+, 19.35
Departs Romeiros: 08.15, 08.45*, 9.20, 10.35•, 11.05*, 11.40, 12.40+, 13.05, 13.35, 14.05, 16.05, 18.10, 18.35+, 19.10, 19.25+. 20.10, 21.10

30 Jardim Botânico ('Largo do Miranda' bus; journey time approx. 15min)
Hourly or every two hours every day of the week.

31 Jardim Botânico (journey time approx. 15min) ■

36 Palheiro Ferreiro ('Lombo da Quinta' bus; journey time approx. 25min) ■
This one terminates 300m/yds below the southern entrance to the Palheiro Gardens.

37 Palheiro Ferreiro (journey time approx. 25min)
Departs Funchal: 07.35, 08.50+, 12.00, 13.10, 16.45, 17.30+, 18.10, 19.20
Departs Palheiro Ferreiro: 12.35, 13.50, 17.40, 18.05+, 18.50, 19.20+, 19.50
Stops at the entrance to the Palheiro Gardens; also at the Levada dos Tornos on the ER102.

45 Funchal • Levada dos Piornais ('Nazaré' bus; journey time approx 10min) ■

47 São João Latrão (journey time approx. 25min)
Departs Funchal: 08.00, 08.50+, 11.00, 12.40, 13.10+, 13.40, 16.05*, 17.20+
Departs São João Latrão (ER201): 11.40, 13.15, 13.40+, 14.10, 16.50*, 18.30

91 Barrreira • Trapiche (shuttle bus; change at Trapiche for Bus 11 or 10A)
Departs Barreira (for Trapiche): 09.45, 12.00, 13.00, 14.00, 14.35, 17.38, 18.11
Departs Trapiche (for Barreira): 09.34, 11.50, 12.39, 13.39, 14.29, 17.32, 18.05

■Services too numerous to list; generally half-hourly (hourly on weekends); *not Sundays or holidays; #not Saturdays; +Mon-Fri; §Sat/Sun/holidays only; •Sundays only

Index

Geographical entries only are included here; for other entries, see Contents, page 3. A page number in **bold type** indicates a photograph; a page number in *italics* a map (*TM* refers to the large-scale walking map on the reverse of the touring map). For pronunciation hints, see page 144. For buses, see Timetables index, page 138.

Abra Bay *see* Baía da Abra
Achada da Pinta 51, 53, *TM*
Achada de Teixeira 14, 26, 27, 89, 91-2, **93**, **108**, *TM*
Achadinha *60-1*, 70, 138
Águas Mansas 22, 59, *62-3*, 71, 138
Arco da Calheta 33, 34, *124-5*
Arco de São Jorge 20, 26, 28
Assomada 13, **16**, 23, *62-3*, 67, 138
Babosas 20, 59, *60-1*, **65**, 138, 142
Baía da Abra 14, 23, *76-7*
Balcões 15, 20, 28, 104, *105*
Barreira *43*, 45-6, 138, 142
Barreiras *54-5*, 58, *114-5*
Bica da Cana 15, 30, 32, 33, **119**, 120, 132, *TM*
Boa Morte 13, 33, *54-5*, **56**, 57, 58, 138
Boaventura 18, 20, **108**, 109, *110*, 138
Boca da Corrida 25, 49, 51, *TM*
Boca do Cerro **48**, 49, 50, *TM*
Boca do Risco 72, 79, *80-1*
Boqueirão 59, *62-3*, 138
Cabo Girão 24, 25, 33, *54-5*, 138
Caldeira *54-5*, 56
Caldeirão do Inferno *98-9*, **100**, **101**, *TM*
Caldeirão Verde 95, *98-9*, *TM*
Calheta 34, *124-5*, 135
Camacha 21, 22, 59, *60-1*, *62-3*, 64, 67, 71, 138
Câmara de Lobos 24
Campanário 34, *54-5*, 57, 138
Campo Grande 122, **123**, *124-5*, *TM*
Canhas 33, 121, 138
Caniçal 23, 72, 74, *76-7*, 138
    road tunnel 23, 72, 74, 75, *76-7*, 79, 80, 138
Caniço 23, *62-3*, 138
Capela dos Cardais 22, *62-3*, 68
Casa do Sardinha *76-7*, 78
Casas do Dr Alberto **51**, *TM*
Cascalho 117, 126, 127, *TM*
Cedro Gordo 28
Chão das Feiteiras 104, *107*
Chão dos Louros 18, 19, 30, *TM*
Choupana *60-1*, 70, 71
Corticeiras 49, 51, 52, *54-5*, 138
Corujeira *114-5*
Cova da Roda 95, 96, *98-9*
Cruz 14, 27, *80-1*, 84-6, 138
Cruz da Caldeira *54-5*, 56
Cruz da Guarda *80-1*, 83, *105*
Cruzinhas 28, 95, **96**, *98-9*, 138
Cumial 92, *TM*
Curral das Freiras 24, **47**, 48, 50, 89, 92, 138, *TM*
Eira de Fora 22
Eira do Mourão *54-5*, **58**
Eira do Serrado 12, 24, 47, 138, *TM*
Eirinha 109, *110*
Encumeada 15, 18, 30, 32, 33, 49,

50, 92, 94, 115, 117, 118, 138, *TM*
Espigão Amarelo **79**, *80-1*, 82
Estreito da Calheta 34
Estreito de Câmara de Lobos 25, 33, 49, *54-5*, 138
Faial 18, 20, 26, 27, 28, 92, 95, 138
Fajã (below Curral) *43*, 44
Fajã (above Ribeira Brava) *54-5*, *114-5*
Fajã da Murta 96, *98-9*
Fajã da Nogueira 28, 100, 101, 102-3, *TM*
Fajã da Ovelha 34, *134-5*
Fajã dos Cardos 92, *TM*
Fanal **8**, *121*
Feiteiras 19, *112*
Florenças *124-5*
Folhadal **117**, 118, *TM*
Fonte do Bispo 30, 31, 33, 137
Fontes 33, 51, 52, 53, 138, *TM*
Formiga 113, *114-5*, 138
Funchal 10-11, **13**, 18, 21, **23**, 24, 26, 33, *43*, 138
Garachico 25, 33, *54-5*, 56, **57**
Gaula *62-3*, 64
Homem em Pé 14, 28, 89, **93**, *98-9*, *TM*
Ilha de São Jorge *98-9*, 110, 138
Jardim da Serra 24, 25, 49, 51
Jardim do Mar *134-5*
João Frino *62-3*, 65
Lamaceiros (above Portela) 70, 71, *98-9*, 104, *105*, 106
Lamaceiros (above Porto Moniz) 31, 136, *137*
Larano 79, *80-1*, 82, 83, 105
Levada 5-7
    Calheta–Ponta do Pargo 125, *134-5*, **135**
    da Bica da Cana 16, *124-5*, 126, **127**, *TM*
    da Central da Ribeira da Janela 16, **136**, *137*
    da Fajã do Rodrigues **19**, **31**, *112*
    da Negra **6**, **39**, *43*, 46, *TM*
    da Portela *80-1*, *105*, 106
    da Ribeira Grande 16, 123, *124-5*, 131
    da Rocha Vermelha *124-5*, 128, 130, **cover**
    da Serra (below Bica da Cana) **119**, 120, *TM*
    da Serra (above Santo da Serra) 14, **21**, 22, 26, 27, 29, *60-1*, *62-3*, 67, 70-1, 104, *105*, *TM*
    das Rabaças **117**, 118, *TM*
    das Vinte e Cinco Fontes 16, 123, *124-5*, 129, 130
    de Cima **108**, 109, *110*
    do Caldeirão Verde 15, 27, 95, **97**, *98-9*, 100-1, 111
    do Caniçal 14, **72**, **73**, **75**, *76-7*, *80-1*

Levada, *continued*
    do Caniço 13, **16**, *62-3*, 67
    do Castelejo 14, *80-1*, 84, *105*
    do Curral (e Castelejo) 41, 42, *43*, **44**, 47, *TM*
    do Furado **2**, 104, *105*, **106**, 107
    do Lombo do Mouro *114-5*, **116**, 119, *TM*
    do Moinho 113, *114-5*
    do Norte 13, 15, 18, 33, *54-5*, **56**, 57-8, 94, **117**, 118, *TM*
    do Paúl 16, **122**, *124-5*, *TM*
    do Pico *60-1*, *62-3*, 71
    do Pico Ruivo *98-9*, 101, **102**, 103, *TM*
    do Risco 16, 123, *124-5*, 128, **129**
    dos Piornais **7**, 12, 41, *43*, **44**
    dos Tornos 13, 22, 26, 59, *60-1*, *62-3*, 64, **65**, 66, 67, 69, 71, 142, *TM*
    Nova (above Faial) *80-1*, 84
    Nova (near Raposeira) *see*
        Levada Calheta–Ponta do Pargo
    Nova (below Santo da Serra) *62-3*, 68, **69**
    Nova (at Tabua) 113, *114-5*
Lombada 12, 41, *43*, 138, 142
Lombada da Ponta do Sol 33, **34**, 113, *114-5*
Lombada dos Marinheiros 135
Lombo do Galego 96, *98-9*
Lombo do Mouro 15, 32, 115, **116**, *TM*
Lombo dos Moinhos *134-5*
Lombo Grande 59, *62-3*, 65, 138
Loreto 33, 122, *124-5*, 128, 135, 138
Lugar da Serra 53
Machico 21-2, *62-3*, **73**, 138
Madalena do Mar 33-4, 138
Maiata *80-1*, *105*
Maroços 22, 72, *80-1*, 138
Miradouro *112*
Miradouro do Juncal 27, *TM*
Montado do Barreiro 26, *TM*
Montado do Pereiro 26
Monte 18, 20, 59, *60-1*, 71, 138, 142
Nogueira 59, *60-1*, *62-3*, **65**, 138
Palheiro Ferriero 21, 22, 26, 59, *60-1*, 63, 138, 142
Paúl da Serra 30, **32**, **116**, 121, *124-5*, 126, 127, 131
Paúl do Mar 33, 34, 133, *134-5*, 138
Penha de Águia 27, *80-1*, **83**, 85-6
Penha de Águia de Baixo *80-1*, 85-6
Pico
    da Cruz 53, *TM*
    da Nogueira 102-3, *TM*
    da Torre 25
    da Urze 32, *124-5*
    das Pedras 26, 27, 95, *98-9*, *TM*
    das Torres **1**, *84-5*, **90-1**, 119, *TM*

143

Pico, *continued*
  do Arco 34
  do Arieiro **1**, **4**, 12, **13**, 14, 18, 20,
    26, 45, **84-5**, **90-1**, **108**, **119**, *TM*
  do Cidrão **90-1**, *TM*
  do Facho 14, 21, 23, 73, 74, *76-7*,
    80, 138
  do Ferreiro 94, *TM*
  do Gato **84-5**, 90, **108**, **119**, *TM*
  do Jorge 94, *TM*
  do Suna 104, *105, 107*, **108**
  dos Barcelos 24, *43*
  Grande **1**, **4**, **48**, 49, 50, **117**, *TM*
  Ruivo **1**, 15, 26, 27, *84-5*, 89, 91,
    92, 93, 100, **119**, *TM*
  Ruivo do Paúl 16, 132, *TM*
Pináculo (Bica da Cana) **119**, 120,
  TM
Pináculo (Funchal) 23
Pinheiro das Voltas 41, 42, *43*, 138,
  142
Poço da Neve 12, **13**, 27, 45, *TM*
Poiso 18, 20, 26, 27, 29, 45, *107*,
  138
Ponta Delgada 18, 19, *110*
Ponta de São Lourenço **14**, 21, 23,
  75, *76-7*, **78**
Ponta do Pargo 33, 34, 135, 138
Ponta do Sol 33, 138
Portela 14, 26, 27, 70, 71, *80-1*, **83**,
  104, *105*, 106, 107, 138
Porto da Cruz 26-7, 79, *80-1*, 82,
  83, 85, 138
Porto Moniz 18, 19, 30, 31, 136,
  137, 138
Prainha *76-7*
Prazeres **15**, 16, 33, 34, 133, *134-5*,
  138
Quebradas (Funchal) 41-2, *43*, 142
Quebradas (above Porto Moniz) 31
Queimadas 15, 26, 27, 89, 95, 97,
  100, 101, 111
Quinta Grande 25, 33, *54-5*, 57
Rabaçal 16, 30, 32, 33, 122, 123,

124-5, 128, **129**, 130, 131
Rancho Pico das Pedras 15, 27, 28,
  95, 97, *98-9*
Raposeira 33, 34, *134-5*, 138
Referta 27, *80-1*, *105*
Ribeira
  Brava *54-5*, **58**, *114-5*, 116
  da Boaventura 13, 22, 23, *62-3*,
    65, **66**
  da Caixa *54-5*, 56, *114-5*, *TM*
  da Fajã da Nogueira 102-3, *TM*
  da Janela 16, 30, 31, 33, *124-5*,
    132, *136*
  da Lapa *43*, 44
  da Maiata *80-1*, 82, 83, *105*
  da Metade 28, **84-5**, *98-9*, *105*
  da Noia **73**, *80-1*
  da Ponta do Sol 113, 117, *114-5*,
    126-7, *TM*
  da Tabua *114-5*
  do Machico 22, *80-1*
  de Santa Cruz *62-3*, 65, 68, **69**
  de Santa Luzia **13**, 45, *TM*
  de São Jorge 29, *88*, *98-9*
  do Alecrim 123, *124-5*, 131
  do Arvoredo 42, *43*
  do Campanário 51, *54-5*, 57, *TM*
  do Curral *43*, 92, *TM*
  do Poço 50, *TM*
  do Poço do Bezerro 104, *105, 107*
  do Porto Novo 13, **16**, 23, *62-3*,
    64, **65**, 67
  do Serrado *75*, *76-7*
  dos Moinhos 109, *110*
  dos Socorridos **7**, 12, 41-2, *43*, **44**
  Grande (Machico) **73**, *80-1*
  Grande (Rabaçal) *124-5*, 129,
    130, **131**
  Seca (Faial) 28, **84-5**, **96**, 100,
    102, 103, *TM*
  Seca (Machico) 73, *80-1*
  Tem-te Não Caias 27, *80-1*, 84,
    105
Ribeira Brava 33, 55, 92, 113, *114-

5*, **116**, 138
Ribeira da Janela 31, *137*
Ribeira da Vaca 135
Ribeira de Machico *80-1*, *105*
Ribeira Seca 72, *80-1*, 138
Ribeirinha *60-1*, *62-3*, 63, 64, **65**,
  67, 138
Ribeiro Frio 15, 18, 20, 26, 28, 104,
  105, *107*, 138
  (river) 28, 84, *105, 107*
Risco 16, *124-5*, 128, **129**
Roçada 109, *110*
Romeiros 59, *60-1*, **65**, 71, 138, 142
Rosário **1**, 18, 19, 30, *112*
Salgados *62-3*, 67
Santa **30**, 31, 138
Santa Cruz 21, 23
Santana 18, 20, 26, 28, **29**, 36, 87,
  88, 89, 92, 95, 97, *98-9*, 100,
  110, 138
Santo da Serra 21, 22, *62-3*, 66, 68,
  69, 71, *80-1*, 138
São Gonçalo **23**
São João Latrão *60-1*, 138, 142
São Jorge 20, 26, 28, **29**, 87, *88*,
  138
São Lourenço, *see* Ponta de
São Martinho *43*
São Paulo 52, *54-5*
São Roque do Faial **84-5**
São Vicente 18, 19, 30, **31**, 115,
  119, 138
Seixal 19, 30
Serra de Água 18, *TM*
Sítio das Quatro Estradas 14, 27,
  59, *62-3*, 66, 68, 69, 71, 107, 138
Tabua 113, *114-5*, *TM*
Terreiro da Luta 26, *60-1*
Torrinhas 89, 92, 94, *TM*
Trapiche *43*, 45, 138, 142
Vale da Lapa *98-9*, 110
Vale do Paraíso 29, *60-1*, 71
Vinte e Cinco Fontes 16, *124-5*,
  128, 130

Pronunciation/translation of some index entries

achada (ah-scháh-dah) small
  plateau
água (áh-gwah) water
arco (áhr-koh) arc or curving
  mountain ridge
baía (bah-ée-ah) bay
baixo (bíe-joh) low
balcões (bahl-kóyngs) balconies
bica (bée-kah) small spring
boca (bóh-kah) mountain pass
  (literally 'mouth')
brava (bráh-vah) wild
cabo (káh-boh) cape
caldeirão (kahl-day-roúngh)
  cauldron, crater, basin
calheta (kahl-yáy-tah) creek
câmara (káh-mah-rah) chamber
caminho (kah-méen-yoh) way,
  path, road
campo (káhm-poh) plain
caniço (kah-née-soh) reed
chão (shoúng) flat place
choupana (show-páh-nah) cottage
corticeiras (kohr-tee-sáy-rahs)
  small cork trees
cova (kóh-vah) pit, cave
cruz (krúj) cross
cruzinhas (kru-zéen-yahs)
  crossroads
curral (koo-ráhl) corral

dentro (déhn-troh) inside
eira (éye-rah) threshing floor
encumeada (in-koo-mee-áh-dah)
  summit with fine views
estanquinhos (esh-tahn-kéen-yohs)
  small ponds
estreito (esh-tráy-toh) the straits
  above
faial (fie-áhl) beech grove
fajã (fah-jáh) small landslide
folhadal (fohl-yah-dáhl) lily-of-the-
  valley tree grove
fonte (fóhn-tay) spring
fora (fóh-rah) outside
janela (jha-náy-lah) window
jardim (jahr-déengh) garden
lamaceiros (lah-mah-sáy-roosh)
  marshy place
lapa (láh-pah) cave, den
levada (leh-váh-dah) watercourse
  (*see* page 6)
lombada (lohm-báh-dah) long
  ridge
lombo (lóhm-boh) ridge separating
  two parallel ravines
miradouro (mee-rah-dóh-roh)
  viewpoint
monte (móhn-teh) mount
mouro (móor-oh) Moor
nogueira (noh-gáy-rah) nut tree

palheiro (pahl-yáy-roh) cow house,
  thatched cottage
paragem (pah-ráh-jengh) bus stop
paúl (pah-óol) marshland
penha (péyn-yah) rocky hill or cliff
pico (pée-koh) peak
poio (póy-oh) terrace
poiso (póy-soh) pause
ponta (póhn-tah) point
portela (pohr-táy-lah) little gateway
porto (póhr-toh) port
prazer (prah-zéhr) pleasure
quebrada (kay-bráh-dah) steep
  slope
queimada (kay-máh-dah) burnt
rabaça (rah-báh-sah) wild celery
recta (ráy-tah) straight (often a
  straight stretch of road)
ribeira (ree-báy-rah) river or river
  valley
risco (réesh-koh) danger
rocha (róh-shah) rock, crag
seixal (sáy-shal) pebbly place
serra (séh-rah) mountain range
sítio (sée-tee-oh) place
torre (tóh-ray) tower
torrinhas (toh-réen-yahs) turrets
vale (váhl) valley
vinhático (veen-yáh-tee-koh)
  indigenous laurel